MURDER
AND
MOUNTAIN JUSTICE
IN THE
MOONSHINE CAPITAL
OF THE WORLD

PHILLIP ANDREW GIBBS

THE
History
PRESS

Published by The History Press
Charleston, SC
www.historypress.com

Front cover, bottom: Courtesy of Special Collections, Virginia Polytechnic & State University; top: Courtesy of the Morris Stephenson Collection.
Back cover: Courtesy of the Morris Stephenson Collection.

First published 2023

Manufactured in the United States

ISBN 9781467153386

Library of Congress Control Number: 2023932163

CONTENTS

CONTENTS

PREFACE

Situated at the southern end of the Great Valley of Virginia near the present-day city of Roanoke, Franklin County encompasses an area of roughly 712 miles and includes the mountains of the Blue Ridge to the west as well as the rolling hills of the Virginia Piedmont in the central and eastern area of the county. Some of the county's highest peaks—Bull Run Knob, Cahas Mountain and Mason's Knob—are well over three thousand feet. The Blue Ridge Parkway, constructed in the 1930s, runs through and along many of these mountains in the western section of the county.

The Blue Ridge Mountains have a wide variety of flora and fauna that are indigenous to the region. Here stand vast forests of oak, poplar, hickory, ash, yellow birch, maple, fir and white pine. The many oak trees that dominate the lower elevations of the Blue Ridge, say biologists, produce isoprene, a hydrocarbon that gives these mountains their distinctive bluish hue. Rhododendron, mountain laurel, dogwood, Queen Anne's lace and black-eyed Susans are just a few of the flowering plants and smaller trees that dot the ridges and meadows. Black bear, white-tailed deer, wild boar, red foxes, bobcats and hundreds of bird and amphibian species have made these ancient mountains their home.

The hardwood and pine forests in the Piedmont and Blue Ridge sections of Franklin County became invaluable to the people of the region, providing not only lumber for homesteads but also a reliable source of income. With the growth of barrel-stave manufacturing in Franklin in the early 1900s and Norfolk and Western Railroad's need for crossties, there was a steady demand for lumber. Farmers like my grandaddy Woods, who were not afraid of hard work, could earn money for their families by logging and operating sawmills in western sections of the county such as Ferrum and Callaway.

The county has plentiful sources of water. The Blackwater and Pigg Rivers run through the central part of Franklin, and well over sixty thousand creeks and streams can be found throughout the county. With names like Maggodee Creek, Roaring Run, Runnett Bag, Polecat Branch and Shooting Creek, these streams provided early settlers and later residents with much-needed cold water for drinking and for springhouses that helped refrigerate eggs, butter and milk. They also teemed with trout, making them a good source for food and recreation.

Later, in the 1950s, two lakes were constructed to prevent flooding and provide hydroelectric power to the county. Both Smith Mountain and Philpott Lake surround Franklin and attract boaters, fishermen, campers and skiers from all over the region and the United States. Although Philpott Lake is overseen by the Army Corps of Engineers and is off-limits to real estate and business development, the environs of Smith Mountain have jumped in population and led to the creation of new communities like that of Westlake in the eastern section of the county.

Despite the county's scenic beauty and abundant natural resources, its citizens, particularly those who lived in the mountain communities of Ferrum, Callaway, Endicott, Runnett Bag and Shooting Creek, often struggled for much of their history to make a living. Their way of life, even well into the twentieth century, was not altogether different from that of their ancestors, largely Scots-Irish immigrants who settled the region in the 1700s. This was especially true of my mother's family.

Born in 1922 to George and Girlie Woods, Winifred Irene and her sister, Thelma, and brother, Posey, lived just off the Six-Mile Post Road on a small farm between Callaway and Ferrum. Not unlike their neighbors, the family lived in a rough-hewn board house that had no running water, electricity or phone service. A creek with a springhouse provided water and cold storage for perishables. A small one-room school, some two miles from their farm, offered children in the community an education up to the seventh grade. There was no bus service, of course, so students had to walk to school.

George Woods, who was respected and, at times, feared by the people in the community, did his best to keep the family fed and clothed. A rather imposing man with a barrel chest and thick gray hair, George Woods worked in timber and plowed his fields with his mules "Kate" and "Doc." Although

The author's maternal grandfather on his Callaway farm with his wagon and beloved mules "Doc" and "Kate." *Courtesy of the author's personal collection.*

he was unable to read or write, he was an intelligent man who kept his own accounts and never shied away from hard work or a fight. He died of a heart attack after putting up hay in his barn on a warm May day in 1958. He was sixty-seven years old.

Years after my grandaddy died and the family farm was sold, we made regular visits to see my granny Girlie Guilliams Woods, who lived with our aunt (always pronounced "ain't" in my family) Lilly Guilliams in the mountains above Ferrum. Granny was born Girlie Gay Guilliams in 1900 and was the oldest in a large family that worked a hardscrabble farm on Ferrum Mountain.

The road to Granny and Aunt Lilly's house was a bit treacherous. The steep climb was paved with large, jagged rocks, and rarely could Daddy's 1959 Ford make the trip without dragging and potentially damaging the oil pan. Most of the time, we just walked the half mile up the mountain, picking blackberries, when in season, along the way. This was not without peril; a copperhead or rattlesnake occasionally interrupted our leisurely walk.

Aunt Lilly was, like Granny Woods, a mountain woman. She raised chickens and pigs, kept milk cows, made butter, quilted and made brooms from sage grass to sweep her floors. It was not unusual that once we arrived at her farmhouse, we saw a dead snake hanging over the fence or a dead crow dangling from one of the several trees in her yard. Aunt Lilly believed that a dead snake positioned strategically over a fence would make it rain. The unfortunate crows that she shot with her .410 shotgun were a warning to any and all winged black devils that a similar fate awaited them if they dared attack her corn.

In later years, she, Granny and my great-uncle Charlie Woods, who was both a player and maker of fiddles and dulcimers, were regular performers and artisans at the annual Blue Ridge Folk-Life Festival at Ferrum College. The festival, together with the Blue Ridge Institute in Ferrum, continues to this day to celebrate and preserve the rich traditions and values that have shaped the society and culture of Franklin County and the region.

One such tradition that figures rather prominently in the annual festival and the institute's exhibits and archives is Franklin County's long history as the most prolific maker of illegal whiskey in the state and perhaps the nation. Carrying on a craft they learned from their Scots-Irish forebearers, mountain families in the county often made whiskey to supplement their meager incomes. Surplus corn and fruit crops, they discovered, could be more profitable when sold in liquid form.

But with the coming of prohibition in Virginia in 1916 and later the passage of the Eighteenth Amendment in 1918, which prohibited the making and sale of alcohol for consumption in the United States, a grand moneymaking opportunity presented itself. Almost overnight, county farmers, including my grandaddy Woods and other kin, began making whiskey.

The market for whiskey seemed insatiable. Moonshine stills dotted the mountain landscape from Ferrum to Callaway, from Endicott to Snow Creek and from Boones Mill to Henry. Impressed by the sheer volume of liquor produced in this corner of the Blue Ridge Mountains during the 1920s, the writer Sherwood Anderson labeled it the "Wettest Spot in the World."

Yet even after the repeal of the Eighteenth Amendment in 1933, there was a strong demand for moonshine in both northern and southern cities. And despite the efforts of federal agents, state ABC (alcohol beverage control) officers and the Sheriff's Department to shut the business down, enterprising county's residents continued to make and run bootleg whiskey—often on a massive scale.

Growing up in Franklin County, I heard tales of bootlegging and bad men. Often as we drove through the mountains to visit my granny Woods and other kinfolk who lived in Ferrum and Callaway, Momma would point out houses, many of them elegant brick Colonial-style homes that resembled the estates that one would might see along the James River of the Virginia Tidewater. She claimed, rather emphatically, that these fine houses were constructed with bootleg money.

Whether they were or were not I never knew. But I did know that Grandaddy Woods and other members of our extended family had at one time or another made illegal whiskey or helped transport it to surrounding towns and cities. Farming in the mountains was difficult and rarely profitable. The lure of ready money, despite the time and work involved and the gamble of getting caught, was hard to resist. Everyone knew there was a market for good mountain whiskey.

Along with the trade in illegal liquor, however, grew a suspicion of authority and the habit of men flouting the law and employing their own notions of justice. Violence and vigilantism, as a consequence, were used to settle disputes, uphold community traditions and values and protect one's family and livelihood. Unsolved homicides, strange disappearances and senseless killings were not uncommon. Such crimes left county sheriffs and commonwealth's attorneys baffled and demoralized.

The chapters that follow are about the good and the not so good people who struggled to make a living in the hills and hollows of Franklin County. Their story is one of poverty, defiance, tragedy and desperation. But their story is also one of sacrifice, fierce independence, courage and intense devotion to family, tradition and justice. And as natives of what became known as the "Moonshine Capital of the World," their story is, in part, my family's story.

ACKNOWLEDGEMENTS

One year before the completion of this book, my best friend James Haynes asked me to write the story of the killing of our friend and classmate Terry Flora. That request led me to investigate not only the murder of Terry but also the long history of violence in our native region—Franklin County, Virginia, and the Blue Ridge Mountains. I was determined to make sure his story, as well as that of others, was told accurately and without prejudice.

I don't think this project would have ever come to fruition without his support and that of my sister, Martha. It was she who made the necessary contacts that enabled me to recount accurately many of the events detailed in this book. It was also she who not only provided me with a place to lay my head but also, on numerous occasions, did the leg work to secure court records and other documents pertinent to the central theme of this work.

It was Denise Willis Young who, however, more than anyone, convinced me to see this endeavor to its end. In interview after interview, she bravely recounted the events of one evening in April 1978 that forever impacted her and her family. The support of this courageous woman for this book has been invaluable. I am, needless to say, in her debt.

There have been so many others that have contributed to this work. Linda Stanley and Ilene Lavender at the Franklin County Historical Society and Ann Copeland and Fran Snead at the Bassett Historical Center provided me with insight and access to a multitude of newspaper articles and other sources that enabled me to document so many of the events that are included in this story. Jamie Mize at the Franklin County Library steered me to sources and helped in reeducating me about the mechanics of microfilm. The staff at the Franklin County Clerk of Circuit Court Office were especially helpful. They took time away from their normal duties to help me locate property transactions, wills and divorce proceedings.

But the list of people who have been essential to this book would not be complete without mentioning Kathy Stephenson, who provided photographs from her father Morris Stephenson's collection of moonshine pictures, or the hard work of John Jackson in the Special Collections Library of Virginia Tech, who, after much searching, found the photograph of the Franklin County Courthouse that appears on the front cover.

And I would be amiss if I didn't thank Kate Jenkins at The History Press for her guidance, insight and attentiveness. She made what could have been an onerous task into an untroublesome endeavor. I was so fortunate to have her and Julia Turner as my editors.

So many of my good friends in Georgia, where I have lived for the past thirty-five years, have also made this work possible. Chris Wharton, my buddy and frequent tennis partner, not only offered words of encouragement but also asked probing questions each time we met for a match about the progress and the layout of the book. And then there is that duo of John Nichols and Kelvin Oliver. They have always shown an unwavering faith in me despite all my flaws. The camaraderie we share on the tennis courts from week to week has added so much to my life.

For me, that life, however, would be empty without music. Over the past eleven years, I have had the privilege of working with three of the finest musicians in the southeastern United States—Donny Screws, Cliff Lee and fellow Virginian Margaret Spielman. Their friendship, together with the music we make together each week as the Midlife Chryslers, has provided me with both a creative and joyous escape from the hard work of researching and writing.

In the end, without the love, support and advice of my wife, Penny, I don't think this book would have ever made it to print. She tolerated my long absences from home, as well as the many days and nights I spent in front of my computer. My only hope is that what follows is equal to the sacrifice.

Chapter 1

A YEAR FOR MURDER

It was Sunday, April 16, 1978, and Terry Flora was excited to show his girlfriend, Denise Willis, just what his new Jeep could do at the soapstone quarry in Henry. Located off Route 605, the abandoned quarry, with its steep hills and dirt trails, was a popular destination for thrill-seeking motorcyclists and four-wheelers. Choosing a path that led to a steep incline, Terry put the Jeep in four-wheel drive, revved the engine and proceeded to make the climb. The Jeep performed beautifully but not without frightening Denise. She was certain the vehicle would flip.[1]

Terry and Denise Willis met through one of her cousins—Bobby Whitlow—who happened to work with Terry at the Burroughs Corporation in Rocky Mount. Denise, not unlike so many in the region, enjoyed traipsing through the woods and was no stranger to guns and hunting and fishing. It was not surprising that she would meet Terry during a deer hunt.[2]

Having a mutual interest in the outdoors, Terry and Denise became fast friends and began dating, albeit with the consent of her parents. It was not long before they were riding together through the woods, down abandoned logging roads and fire lanes in Franklin and Henry Counties. They were having the time of their lives and planned to get married after she turned eighteen and graduated high school. In fact, he had given her a pre-engagement ring. He was twenty-one; she, fifteen.[3]

Not wanting to miss Denise's 11:00 p.m. curfew, the two later left the quarry and headed down the main road for the return trip to her house in Oak Level. It was soon after that they noticed a two-tone Cadillac following

Terry Flora and Denise Willis near the time of their confrontation with Jaybird Philpott in April 1978. *Courtesy of Denise Willis Young.*

them. To their surprise, the driver flashed his lights on and off, signaling them to stop. Uncertain as to what the folks in the Cadillac wanted, Denise told Terry not to stop.[4]

But Terry thought that perhaps the driver was alerting them to some problem with the Jeep or there was a medical emergency and pulled over. A slight, balding man who was well into his fifties got out of the Cadillac. As the man approached the Jeep, both Terry and Denise could see that there was a woman sitting in the passenger seat of the Cadillac. Visibly irate, the

14

man claimed that they were trespassing and demanded that Terry tell him his name. Terry said he had no idea that he was trespassing and was not about to give him his name. This only made the man even angrier, so much so that he opened the door and pulled Terry out of the vehicle. What happened next would set in motion a series of events that would change their lives as well as those of their families.[5]

The man pushed Terry and began to pummel him. The man was clearly more than thirty years his senior, and Terry backed away, yelling repeatedly that he was not going to fight him. But the older man was relentless and charged Terry, bringing him to the ground. Now with the man on top of him, he had no choice but to defend himself. Fearing for his life, Terry yelled for Denise to get the gun—a .22-caliber pistol he often kept on the rear floorboard of the Jeep. She looked frantically for the pistol, but it was dark; she couldn't find it.[6]

By this time, the man left his struggle with Terry, and seeing that the Jeep door was open, he reached in and tried to grab the keys. It now became clear that he planned to do Denise harm. She fought the man and managed to kick him out of the Jeep. The woman who accompanied the man now had gotten out of the car and was standing next to the vehicle. Hysterical, she yelled, "Jay, Jay, Stop!"[7]

Seconds later, she saw Terry standing with his back to the open door and facing the man. Now wielding a knife, he lunged at Terry, who then suddenly fell to the ground. The woman screamed, "We've got to go!" and pulled the man back to the car. As the couple sped away, Terry crawled into the driver's seat of the Jeep but said he had been stabbed, and Denise would have to drive and get help.[8]

Denise quickly got out and went around to the driver's side. Terry slumped into the passenger's seat, and she got in. She knew how to drive, but she had never operated a manual transmission. As she hurriedly tried to figure out the mechanics of the clutch and gears, Terry fell into her lap, unconscious.[9]

Once she got the vehicle moving, she remembered that her cousin Bobby Whitlow lived four miles down the road. Terry lay in her lap the entire way. When they arrived, Bobby managed to get Terry into the house and called for medical help. But it was too late; Terry was dead. They would later learn from the autopsy report that the man's knife had punctured his heart.[10]

The sheriff of Franklin County, Quinton Overton, and his deputies, along with the coroner, arrived soon after. They asked Denise what she had witnessed and later took her to the Sheriff's Department in Rocky Mount to look at mug shots of men who could have possibly been responsible for

This was the red-and-white Cadillac that Jaybird Philpott was driving the evening he stabbed Terry Flora. The police found it in the field behind his house. Bloodstains were discovered in the interior. *Courtesy of the* Franklin News Post.

stabbing Terry. Overton and her father, B.B. Willis, stood by as she flipped through the photographs. Suddenly, her eyes widened. "This is the man!" she exclaimed.

Overton and her father looked at one another worriedly. It was William Jefferson "Jaybird" Philpott.[11]

When deputies went to Jaybird's house in Henry, Jaybird said he knew nothing about the stabbing and that he had been at home all evening. When he was told that the couple who confronted Terry and Denise were driving a red-and-white vehicle that fit the description of his Cadillac, he claimed that he had allowed a friend to borrow the car that evening and perhaps he would know something about the incident. Jaybird, however, refused to divulge the name of the man.[12]

Convinced that he was lying, Quint Overton and his deputies combed the area for the vehicle. Having no luck, they called in a state police helicopter to conduct an aerial search. They eventually spotted the Cadillac in a field below his house. An inspection of the car turned up bloodstains on the seats. Jaybird was arrested and brought back to the Sheriff's Department. But he would not remain there long. Lloyd Foley, a friend and Ferrum sawmill owner, posted the $75,000 bond for his release.[13]

A notorious moonshiner, Jaybird Philpott was well known to the authorities. He had a reputation for violence and was suspected in the murder of his first wife. Knowing what Jaybird was capable of, Sheriff Overton decided to put Denise immediately into protective custody. Officers would be assigned to her home, and plans were made to put her in a safe house far away from Jaybird and anyone he might contract to kill her.[14]

Quentin Overton served as sheriff of Franklin County from 1976 to 1988. He knew what Jaybird Philpott was capable of and that Denise Willis should be placed in protective custody. *Courtesy of the Roanoke Times.*

~ ~ ~ ~ ~ ~ ~

FIVE MONTHS LATER, ON Monday, September 4, the Sheriff's Department received a call about a murder at a trailer on Route 766, roughly four miles from Ferrum. When Quint Overton and his deputies arrived, James and Janet Perdue directed them to the bedroom of Ivan Young, a sixty-four-year-old partially blind man, who shared the trailer with them. Inside, they found Young sprawled on the bed—dead with three gunshots to his head.[15]

According to the Perdues, they left to go fishing at Smith Mountain Lake around 2:00 p.m. They invited Young to join them, but he declined the invitation. When they left, Young was sitting outside the trailer with a gun across his arm. Young, they said, seemed to live in fear that someone was going to kill him. Janet Perdue said that he had told her that he had killed a man several years ago and had a lot of enemies. He always slept, she said, with as many as four guns in his bed and believed revenge could have been the motive for the killing.[16]

While Young's partial blindness (caused by a gunshot wound to his head when he was seventeen) had prevented him from securing steady work in the county's factories and sawmills, it did not stop him from finding a source of income. He was well known to have operated moonshine stills for many years in the area, and on the day of his murder, he had a considerable amount of money stashed in his bedroom.[17]

This possibly, thought Overton, could have been the motive for the murder. All of Young's money was missing, said the Perdues, except seventeen dollars. Two of his guns also could not be located.[18]

Dr. David Oxley, the state medical examiner, performed an autopsy on Young's body and determined that he had died from gunshots from a small-caliber pistol at close range. The report convinced Overton that this was not a theft or even a revenge killing. The Perdues, he believed, knew more than they were telling.[19]

~ ~ ~ ~ ~ ~ ~

On the morning of Tuesday, October 17, Sheriff Overton received a call from a Boones Mill man about a young Black woman's body he discovered lying on the doorstep of his elderly brother's home. When the sheriff arrived on the scene, he found a woman who appeared to be in her twenties, dead, apparently from several shotgun blasts. The owner of the home said he heard someone beating on his door the night before and then two shots. Afraid to open the door, he retreated to his bedroom and fell asleep. It was only when his brother came by to check on him the following morning that they found her.[20]

Overton and his deputies could locate nothing on the woman or nearby that would help identify her. But they did find footprints that led through a wooded area roughly two-tenths of a mile from the house. The prints indicated that she perhaps was running for help. Tire tracks found in the vicinity suggested that she had been in a car with her killer or killers and managed to escape. Overton believed they then chased her in the car within 120 feet of the elderly man's house and opened fire.[21]

After several inquiries in the area, Overton learned that she looked like a woman who had been living with a couple of migrant workers who were picking apples in a Boones Mill orchard. The owner of the orchard, Clark Jamison, believed she had left the orchard with the workers the Saturday before her body was discovered. Jamison said the men were good workers and caused no trouble. He wasn't sure where they had gone, but Overton believed they were headed to Winchester to work the apple orchards there.[22]

A few days after the woman's murder, an acquaintance came forward and identified her as Betty Lou Hancock, twenty-five, of Roanoke. She wasn't married, appeared to have no family in the area and had no place of residence or employment. She was, however, often seen in the market area of downtown Roanoke. Overton and his deputies were perplexed as to what could have possibly been the motive for her murder. The answer, they concluded, lay with the two migrant workers.[23]

~ ~ ~ ~ ~ ~ ~

ON THE EVENING OF October 19, Bill McGhee looked at the clock and began to wonder where his sons Milton and Larry were. It was late, and he had supper waiting for them. No doubt they were hungry. They had been working all day at a logging site just off of 619 not far from Ferrum. It was getting dark; surely, they weren't still cutting and loading timber. Around 7:00 p.m., he decided that he should check on them.[24]

When Bill got to the site, he saw no sign of Milton, Larry or their coworker Jimmy Moran. He yelled for the boys but heard nothing in reply. Believing they must have already left, he drove back to his house in Waidsboro. Still no word from his sons. It was now late in the evening; something was definitely wrong.[25]

Returning to the site, he decided to search the area. With just a single flashlight, it was hard to see much of anything—that is, until he caught a glimpse of a shadowy figure on the hydraulic log loader. As he got closer, he could now see that it was Milton. He had been shot dead.[26]

Frightened and in shock, he hurried home and called Sheriff Overton. He told the sheriff that his eldest son, Milton, had been killed, and he had no idea where Larry and Jimmy were. Sheriff Overton told Bill to meet him at a store near Waidsboro on Route 40. From there, they drove to the logging site. But as they headed down the one-lane logging road, they saw a car moving toward them in the opposite direction. Not sure if the driver was involved in the killing, the sheriff stopped his vehicle and got out. He then drew his pistol and ordered the driver to stop. It was one of the McGhees' relatives who was trying to help Bill find his sons.[27]

Sheriff Overton called his deputies to the scene. Working by flashlight, they found Larry and Jimmy. Lying roughly 135 yards from Milton, Jimmy was discovered near a bulldozer with a shotgun blast to his back and then another to his head. Beside him lay Larry. He had been forced to kneel and was shot at almost point-blank range.[28]

Overton asked the medical examiner Dr. David Oxley to do an autopsy of the bodies. The autopsy results revealed that Milton McGhee, thirty-two; Larry McGhee, twenty-three; and Jimmy Moran, twenty, had been killed sometime in the midafternoon on Thursday, October 19, 1978. Each had sustained head wounds, he concluded, with a twelve-gauge shotgun. Quint Overton commented to the *Franklin News-Post* that the execution-style killing of the McGhees and Moran was unlike any murder he had ever investigated in the county: "This murder was calculated and cold-blooded....I have been in law enforcement for 19 years and I have never seen anything like this. I do not believe there has ever been a more savage killing in Franklin County." Everyone in the county—Dr. Oxley, sheriff's deputies and citizens—seemed to agree that "the triple murder was one of the most vicious and brutal murders in Franklin County history."[29]

Although the county was no stranger to violence and lawlessness, particularly in the moonshining areas of Ferrum, Runnett Bag, Shooting Creek and Endicott, these murders stunned its citizens. Men who were accustomed to working in remote logging sites, now carried pistols and shotguns out of fear that they might suffer the same fate as the McGhees and Moran. People who had felt reasonably secure in their homes now made sure doors were bolted and windows closed and locked. According to Sheriff Overton, people who might have leads to the slayings would not speak to him on the telephone. "I have to drive out and speak to them," said Overton, "because they are afraid."[30]

~ ~ ~ ~ ~ ~ ~

IN DECEMBER, THAT FEAR and unease was compounded in Ferrum when two rabbit hunters' dogs led them to a burned-out car on a hillside pine thicket about seven miles south of the town off Route 767. Inside the car were two charred bodies. Sheriff Overton, who was called to the scene, reported that the bodies were so severely burned that he "couldn't tell if they were male or female or white or black." What he could tell, however, was that this certainly was no accident. The two, he believed, had been murdered.[31]

After removing the bodies, Overton, his deputies and the medical examiner immediately began the search for their identities as well as the owner of the car. Although the fire had destroyed the car's license plates, they were able to locate its engine identification number and trace it to the owner. The owner, however, could not be found, and Sheriff Overton declined to give his name.[32]

Dr. Oxley performed the autopsy and was able to positively identify the two bodies. Using dental records, he revealed that the victims were Robert Alexander Newbill, twenty, of Rocky Mount and David Dodd Hagerstrom, twenty-three, of Bristol, Tennessee. The two young men, he also said, had been shot before they were burned, thus confirming Overton's suspicions. Both Newbill and Hagerstrom were former Ferrum College students. The car was registered to Robert Newbill.[33]

Was this murder connected to the October murders? After all, Newbill and Hagerstrom were found only seven miles from the site where the McGhees and Moran had been killed. But given the identity of the victims, the forensic evidence and the attempt to destroy their bodies, Sheriff Overton didn't think so. Nevertheless, there was cause for concern. The murder rate for Virginia in 1977 was 9 per 100,000 people. With a population of only 35,000, Franklin County would match that number of homicides in 1978. It was truly a year for murder.[34]

Chapter 2

HARD SPIRITS, DEFIANT SOULS

eople like the Philpotts, McGhees, Willises and my own family who lived in the western sections of Franklin County and the Blue Ridge are descended from the Lowland Scots who settled Northern Ireland in the seventeenth century. Beginning in the early 1600s, these hardy farmers and herdsmen immigrated to Northern Ireland with the intention of settling the area for James I. James hoped that these fierce Presbyterians would establish a bulwark against Catholicism and weld the island closer to England and its institutions. In turn, they were promised inexpensive land to rent on Ulster Plantation, the collective name for the estates that James confiscated from Irish noblemen. They were also assured that they would be free to worship as they pleased.[35]

But when rents increased and the Church of England demanded that they recognize its preeminence, they began leaving Ulster for North America. Between the 1720s and '60s, they came by the thousands. Arriving first at the port of Philadelphia, they traveled south following what came to be known as the "Great Wagon Road." That road led to an area known to Native Americans as "Big Lick," the present-day location of the city of Roanoke. Following what is today Route 220 and Route 11, they moved farther south and west searching for good, arable land.[36]

Making up the largest percentage of settlers in Southwestern Virginia, they played a significant role in shaping the culture of Franklin County, particularly its more mountainous areas. In the hills of Endicott, Ferrum, Callaway and Henry, for example, they established farms, raised livestock,

The Ulster Scots who settled much of Franklin County carried their worldly possessions in Conestoga wagons south from Philadelphia through the Great Valley of Virginia and into the Blue Ridge Mountains during the early to mid-eighteenth century. The path they followed came to be known as the Great Wagon Road. *Courtesy of the Library of Congress.*

hunted and trapped and fished the numerous creeks and streams. It was here too that they made fiddles and dulcimers to play the ballads and reels that they had known in Ireland and Scotland. At community events like weddings, "corn shuckings," "barn raisings" and "wood gettings," this "string music," as it was known, filled the air. And to songs such as "Sally Goodin," "Cripple Creek" and "Pretty Polly," they flatfooted late into the evening.[37]

Whiskey, the favorite drink of the Ulster Scots and their descendants in Franklin County, was ever present at such gatherings. But the whiskey that their ancestors made and drank in Scotland and Northern Ireland was distilled largely from wheat. Finding wheat and other grains often difficult to grow in the mountains, they began planting corn and used it to make liquor. By the late eighteenth century, corn whiskey became not only the most common drink for mountain people but also an important source of their income.[38]

Following the American Revolution, the newly established government, under the direction of Secretary of the Treasury Alexander Hamilton, decided that distillers of whiskey should pay an excise tax. The imposition of the "Whisky Tax" was anathema to these people and led to a rebellion in western Pennsylvania and some western counties of Virginia. While the

Whiskey Rebellion largely fizzled after government troops, led by President George Washington, entered Pennsylvania to suppress the uprising, farmers and other enterprising citizens continued to distill whiskey with no intention of paying a tax.[39]

This defiance of the law was not born in the hills and hollows of Virginia or Pennsylvania. On the contrary, the Ulster Scots had long evaded British tax collectors by fashioning small stills that they could carry on their backs and move from place to place to avoid detection. This also gave rise to the name "moonshine," since the liquor was often made in the cover of darkness.[40]

Just like their ancestors, law or no law, mountain people in Virginia refused to pay taxes on distilled whiskey. But fortunately, they had a friend in Thomas Jefferson. After defeating John Adams and the Federalist political party in the election of 1800, Thomas Jefferson and the Democratic Republicans repealed the hated whiskey tax and freed distillers from what they saw as an impediment to their livelihood and personal liberty.[41]

With the exception of a brief imposition of a tax to support the War of 1812, the federal government left whiskey distillers alone in the first half of the nineteenth century. As a result, small home distilleries and larger concerns flooded the country with hard whiskey. During this period, whiskey was so abundant that taverns sprang up in every small village and town to quench the thirst of local inhabitants. By the eve of the Civil War, much of the country's population, young and old, male and female, had developed a daily habit of consuming strong spirits.[42]

It's estimated that Americans, particularly those in the South, during the antebellum period consumed the equivalent of ten gallons of hard whiskey and brandy a year. Colonial Americans did consume wine, English ale, beer and rum, but it was the Scots-Irish and their long tradition of distilling strong spirits that changed Americans' drinking habits. Whiskey became Americans' preferred spirit.[43]

Whiskey consumption became associated with manliness. During extended hunting and fishing trips, card games or sporting events, men challenged one another to drinking contests—often with tragic consequences. While playing cards with several men, Charles F. Snead, a resident of Long Branch in Franklin County, declared that he could drink a gallon of whiskey. "One of the men," it was reported in the *Richmond Times Dispatch*, "threw a dollar on the table, and told him it was his property if he would drink a pint of whiskey." Snead drank the whiskey, played another round of cards and then began the walk home. "He fell unconscious on the way," said the article, "and died in a few minutes."[44]

Men drank large quantities of liquor at community events and celebrations. During local musters, men would drill and hone their shooting skills while consuming whiskey—a lethal combination that occasionally led to fatal accidents. Overindulgence also contributed to violent confrontations at political events. Political rallies, debates and elections were well attended during the nineteenth century, and candidates often plied voters with whiskey, brandy and hard cider.[45]

Politicians and those charged with law enforcement and administering justice fell victim to the allure of whiskey and were unable to carry out their duties. In 1880, concerned citizens in Franklin County asked the General Assembly to remove Judge Thomas B. Claiborne from the bench. According to their petition, Judge Claiborne was unfit for office. He had "no knowledge of courts and their proceedings as is even ordinarily possessed by justices, sheriffs, and other county officers."

Worse yet, the judge "often gets drunk, often drinking to excess in term time—so as of itself to render him unfit for the discharge of his duties as judge." Judge Claiborne was "often seen on the streets of Rocky Mount drunk and disorderly." He also was known for "carrying concealed weapons" and running "unlawful gaming" in his courtroom. Given the charges against him, Judge Claiborne decided to resign.[46]

This culture of consuming "ardent spirits" impacted families. Men who habitually drank to excess often were unable to work and provide for their wives and children. Many became abusive and brutalized their family members. Others died from cirrhosis of the liver or alcohol-related accidents.[47]

Alarmed by the prevalence of hard drinking in America and its deleterious effect on families and public morality, ministers and middle-class women, largely in the northeastern United States, began organizing temperance societies. The Woman's Christian Temperance Union, for example, was born in the 1830s with the goal of encouraging men to abstain from drinking alcohol or at least temper their drinking. Out of this movement would grow a larger crusade in the late nineteenth century to ban altogether the making of alcohol for consumption.[48]

While Virginians would later come to embrace temperance and eventually a ban on alcohol in the early 1900s, for most of the nineteenth century such crusades were dismissed in the South. Drinking was very much associated with good living and hospitality. And for those who lived in the Blue Ridge in Virginia, such efforts were an affront to their way of life. Hard spirits were not only widely consumed; they were also distilled for profit. Any attempt to ban them or tax the making of them would be met with fierce resistance.[49]

During the second year of the Civil War, Abraham Lincoln decided, however, that much-needed revenue to fund the war effort could be gained with the revival of a tax on distilled spirits. The Confederate government at the same time decided to ban the distillation of whiskey, since corn, wheat and barley were needed to feed soldiers at the front. Once more, the copper and other metals used in the construction of stills could be diverted for use in the production of armaments.[50]

Despite support for the Confederate cause, mountain folk in Virginia resisted the law and continued to make whiskey. Whether it was the federal government or the Confederacy, the citizens of Virginia counties like Franklin were not going to allow any law or government agency to interfere with their efforts to make a living. And so, the whiskey continued to flow.

~ ~ ~ ~ ~ ~ ~

FOLLOWING THE CIVIL WAR, whiskey makers in Franklin County increased their production. Times were hard. Farmers in Virginia and even those throughout the nation had difficulty making ends meet. Prices for wheat and corn remained low, and a deflated currency made money scarce. Corn, concluded farmers in Franklin County, was more profitable in liquid than solid form.[51]

Intent on enforcing the tax on distilled whiskey, federal and state authorities sought to shut down bootleggers in the one Virginia county that seemed to harbor the most flagrant violators of the law. Franklin County moonshiners,

Turnip stills, so named for their resemblance to a turnip bulb, date back centuries and were in common use from the mid-1700s through the 1930s in the Blue Ridge Mountains. *Courtesy of* Archaeology Magazine.

they discovered, were producing massive quantities of untaxed liquor with little or no interruption. Federal agents estimated that thousands of gallons of whiskey were being distilled and making their way to the surrounding cities.[52]

Efforts on the part of state and federal revenue officers to shut down these operations were met with violence at every turn during the late nineteenth century and the early 1900s. In February 1884, a mounted band of officers traveled to the western section of the county with the intention of capturing a band of moonshiners who had been operating for some time with blatant disregard for the law. But the officers were easily detected, and the moonshiners were prepared to resist any attempt to destroy their stills or capture them. When the officers demanded that they surrender unconditionally, they were met, according to the *Richmond Dispatch*, with a fusillade of gunfire:

> *This* [gunfire] *was answered by a volley from the Winchester rifles and revolvers of the attacked party. Two of the officers were wounded and two more had their horses killed under them. A ball passed through the hair of another. The revenue officers were forced to beat a hasty retreat and leave the moonshiners in possession of the field. Another and larger force will be sent after the outlaws. They are well armed and so well fortified in the mountain fastnesses as almost to defy capture.*[53]

Although determined to bring Franklin County bootleggers to justice, revenue officers were clearly outfoxed, outnumbered and outgunned. And given the sheer number of people making and drinking untaxed whiskey, officers found county citizens and local authorities unwilling to assist them.

This was evident when a "revenue gang," as described by the *Franklin Gazette*, invaded and occupied the home of a local bootlegger. Indignant that revenue agents would destroy a man's still—that is, his personal property—the editors of the *Gazette* condemned the revenue officers and their "diabolical work" and fully supported the mountain men who came to the aid of their neighbor:

> *The news of the invasion had spread and the sturdy mountaineers, armed with their unerring rifles, had gathered from far and near. The house was surrounded. Their horses, tied near, were shot and killed, and the revenue-men were paralyzed with fright. If one ventured to come from under the bed a rifle spoke and a hissing bullet admonished him to get back. This state of things lasted all day, the man whose property they had destroyed standing between them and deserved punishment.... They sneaked home on foot and those who have seen them pronounce their hair three shades lighter, and say their faces still wear a frightened look.*[54]

Few Franklin County citizens, including local authorities and newspaper editors, were willing to cooperate with revenue officers. Their presence in the county was regarded as an unwarranted intrusion into the efforts of hardworking men to make a living for their families.

During the early 1900s, revenue officers invaded Blue Ridge communities in an effort to shut down illegal distilling. *Courtesy of the Library of Congress.*

As a consequence, aggressive revenue officers, hell-bent on enforcing the law, could find themselves targeted for assassination. In December 1912, Andre Edmundson, a revenue officer conducting investigations of illegal distilling in the western sections of the county, received an anonymous letter telling him the whereabouts of three barrels of whiskey and a still in Waidsboro. When Edmundson reached the spot the following day, he found no whiskey or a still, but he did discover that he had been set up for an ambush. Standing behind a tree, a man with a shotgun opened fire on Edmundson. The blast hit Edmundson's hand as he reached for his pistol. He managed, however, to exchange fire with his would-be assassin and pursue him through the woods: "Wounded though he was, the officer gave chase for more than a quarter mile, and the two men did battle until all of their ammunition was exhausted. Mr. Edmundson then had to walk four or five miles until he could get a horse to finish his journey home."[55] J.P. Hodges, the sheriff at the time, organized a posse and arrested Bernard Stanley. Stanley had previously threatened Edmundson for seizing illegal whiskey that he had found on his farm near Waidsboro.[56]

28

Earlier, in 1890, revenue officers were met with fierce resistance when they tried to shut down an armed mountain camp of over two hundred moonshiners who had more than one hundred stills in operation. Situated on top of a mountain near Shooting Creek and Runnett Bag, these bootleggers were well organized and had spies positioned at the precipice to alert them to the approach of revenue officers. But according to the *Shenandoah Herald*, they were also a well-outfitted army: "They are well equipped for offensive and defensive operations. They are armed with the latest breech-loading rifles, shotguns, and revolvers. They have built a small fort and are in position to stand a long siege. It is stated on good authority that they have recently mounted two or three cannon in the fort."[57] This army of moonshiners, said observers, was composed of "exconvicts, desperadoes, murderers, and the most daring and desperate cut-throats ever collected together."[58]

After having repulsed several attempts to overtake the camp, the men inside had little fear that they would be captured and their operations shut down. In fact, it was reported that they had complete control of the western section of the county, and anyone not known to them was guarded and not permitted to go anywhere alone until they were out of their territory. Officers believed it would take a force of two hundred men to capture the camp and destroy the stills.[59]

But the Treasury Department did not have the funds to equip the small army necessary to shut down moonshining in Franklin County. And even if funds were available, county citizens were not inclined to help revenue agents either because they too were connected to the business or they feared reprisals from bootleggers. Needless to say, conscientious revenue officers were frustrated:

> *There is more or less danger to those who render revenue officers assistance. Many instances can be cited where a man has had his house or barn burned simply because they gave him something to eat or allowed them to sleep in his house for one night: It is very difficult for a revenue officer, if he is known, to obtain shelter or food in many of the country districts.*[60]

While there may have been some in the county who would like to see the moonshiners shut down and the lawlessness abated, few were willing to cooperate with revenue agents.

Nevertheless, despite local resistance and limited funding, revenue officers pursued moonshiners and broke up their operations wherever they found them. In the spring of 1912, revenue officers destroyed a number of distilling

This 1911 Rand McNally map shows the location of Endicott, Shooting Creek and Henry, some of the most prolific moonshining communities in Franklin County. *Courtesy of Rand McNally.*

operations in the mountains near Callaway and Nowlin's Mill. But because people in the community raised the alarm whenever revenuers or anyone suspicious approached, moonshiners were often able to escape and avoid arrest. Such was the case in the Callaway raid. As the agents made their way into the mountains, people in the community "heralded in advance by telephone and the moonshiners throughout the mountains were warned by ringing bells and the discharge of dynamite."[61]

Although whiskey making in Callaway would be interrupted, most moonshiners were able to run deep into the mountains with valuable parts of their stills and avoid capture: "Fires were put out and the stills taken from their flues and hidden in the mountains in many instances. One man took his copper still on his back and hurried across the mountain, pursued by the officers, and was forced to drop it in order to make good his own escape."[62] Over a two-day period, the revenue agents successfully cut up fifteen stills and dumped thousands of gallons of mash, but they made no arrests. Their quarry had escaped and, in a matter of weeks, would return to renew their operations.

Chapter 3

THE WETTEST SPOT

On the evening of October 31, 1916, thousands of people gathered at churches and in the streets of Richmond and other cities to celebrate the death of John Barleycorn in Virginia. By referendum, a majority of its citizens had approved in 1914 the statewide prohibition of alcohol. In response, the General Assembly passed a statute implementing prohibition beginning November 1, 1916. The *Richmond Times Dispatch* reported that "1800 friends of prohibition at the Grace Street Baptist Church did not go home till morning pausing for a moment at midnight to listen to the tooting of whistles and the pealing of church bells and to sing 'Praise God From Whom All Blessings Flow,' and then going on with the speech making."[63]

In speech after speech, ministers, leaders of the Anti-Saloon League of Virginia, the Woman's Prohibition League of America, members of the General Assembly and a stream of state leaders praised the righteous work of those assembled. Each echoed the sentiments of Lieutenant Governor J. Taylor Ellyson.

> *I hazard the prophecy that the talk of the opponents of reform that prohibition would not prohibit would prove false. Virginians are a law-abiding people. There are thousands who did not want prohibition who will aid in enforcing the law....I am sure Virginia will teach other states that here prohibition will prohibit.*[64]

He concluded that "the day is not far distant when not only Virginia, but all of the states will be free of the domination of Rum."[65]

The adoption of prohibition in Virginia was particularly sweet for James Cannon, an educator and bishop of the Southern Methodist Church. For years, Cannon, as superintendent of the Virginia Anti-Saloon League and a loyal Democrat, had lobbied the party to embrace prohibition. Although there had been much resistance from party leaders, they eventually relented and supported the cause, albeit grudgingly. Following the victory in Virginia, Bishop Cannon turned his attention to other states and began the campaign for the passage of the Eighteenth Amendment.[66]

Bishop James Cannon worked feverishly to bring about prohibition in Virginia. His efforts paid off in 1916, when a statewide referendum empowered the Virginia General Assembly to ban the distilling of alcohol in the state. *Courtesy of the Encyclopedia of Virginia.*

Meanwhile, liquor and wine dealers in Richmond and the state struggled to keep pace with the endless stream of customers who wanted to purchase as much wine, beer, bourbon and gin as possible before the statute went into effect. "All day long," reported the *Times Dispatch*, "express wagons, moving vans, and emergency carriers delivered liquor and wine assignments to addresses in every part of the city." By midafternoon, the inventory of most of the city's largest liquor dealers was exhausted. Signs outside saloons and taverns that featured draft beer announced that their kegs were empty.[67]

The Mountain Rose Distillery near Henry, one of the largest legal whiskey makers in Franklin and Henry Counties, told its customers that they needed to prepare for prohibition. Good whiskey would be hard to find, its advertisements said, and everyone should place their orders immediately. The holidays were fast approaching, and quality corn whiskey would not be available.[68]

After much debate over who should be charged with enforcing the ban on alcohol in the state, the General Assembly decided to create a prohibition commissioner. The commissioner would be given "wide powers in running down and convicting violators of the law, having authority to appoint as many deputies as he may deem necessary for the conduct of his office, all of them vested with the powers of sheriffs of the Commonwealth." The members elected Reverend J. Sidney Peters to serve as the new commissioner.[69]

Peters, a Methodist minister and co-owner of two "dry" newspapers, had actively worked with Bishop Cannon's Anti-Saloon League and other prohibition organizations to bring about the statewide ban on alcohol. Given his close connections to the Anti-Saloon League, many wondered whether he would be an independent and impartial enforcer of the law. After all, the commissioner's offices were located in the old headquarters of the Anti-Saloon League in Richmond. No one, however, questioned his enthusiasm or his devotion to the task of enforcement. He was determined to keep Virginia dry and promote morality and Christian virtues.[70]

~ ~ ~ ~ ~ ~ ~

THE ADOPTION OF PROHIBITION in Virginia in 1916 and later the entire nation in 1918 did little to slow whiskey making in Franklin County. On the contrary, the ban on liquor presented a grand moneymaking opportunity, and soon, moonshine stills dotted the mountain landscape from Ferrum to Callaway, from Endicott to Snow Creek and from Boones Mill to Henry. Everyone was in the business of making liquor, including my own grandaddy Woods and other kinfolk in Franklin County.

Struck by the sheer volume of liquor produced in this corner of the Blue Ridge Mountains in the late 1920s, President Hoover's Wickersham Commission in 1930 labeled it "the wettest spot in the nation." Frederick C. Dezendorf, the attorney for the Federal Prohibition Bureau, reaffirmed the conclusions of the commission. According to Dezendorf, "ninety-nine out of 100 persons residing in Franklin County are making or have some connection with illicit liquor." The Virginia attorney general, together with the Franklin County sheriff and commonwealth's attorney, disagreed with this assessment. Only 10 percent of the county's citizens, they argued, had anything to do with making bootleg whiskey.[71]

Dezendorf's statement was, no doubt, an exaggeration. But for Prohibition agents on the ground in Franklin County, it didn't seem far off the mark. William B. Pickerel, a federal Prohibition agent who made numerous raids on stills in the Henry and Philpott sections of the county, expressed his frustration in an article to the *Covington Virginian* in 1926. According to Pickerel, his and his fellow officers' efforts were futile given the number of people and the amount of money involved in the business. He suspected that a "syndicate is financing the liquor making in Franklin County and in the Philpott neighborhood for all the sensational raids have been made there and new stills spring up as fast as the officers mow them down."[72]

Breaking up stills was doing little to stop the river of whiskey that flowed out of the county. Exasperated, federal and state officers decided on a new line of attack. Peters's chief revenue agent in Virginia, S.R. Brame, said that he would "root out the evil at its foundation head by seizing all shipments of meal, malt, yeast copper, and copper tubing and other materials that he has a reasonable belief go into the making of 'moonshine liquor.'" Brame made good on his promise. In July 1920, his agents seized and destroyed $1,500 worth of malt that they found in Ferrum.[73]

Both state and federal Prohibition agents also seized livestock that were connected to moonshining operations. During a raid on a still site near Henry in Franklin County, agents discovered that four hogs, a sow and a litter of pigs were being fed the runoff from the mash. The pigs, said the agents, enjoyed the slop and were in "prime condition." But what were they to do with them? Since "they were a prime factor in the consumption of the by-products of the moonshining operation," they decided to confiscate them. But at the time, they had no way of transporting them. They finally decided to cut off the tails of the guilty hogs so that they could be identified later when they had means to deliver them to their offices in Danville.[74]

Peters and Brame's vigorous enforcement of Prohibition also included encouraging officers to fire on moonshiners who failed to surrender to authorities. In July 1920, moonshiner Posey Thomas was killed when Officer Wood attempted to stop him while driving a car loaded with sixty gallons of liquor between Franklin and Patrick Counties. According to the officers, "Thomas who after a struggle with Wood perched on the running board of the liquor car tore himself loose and leaped out on the other side of the car." As Thomas fled from the scene, officers said he fired on them. In self-defense, they returned the fire. Thomas was later found in a cornfield dead with a bullet wound to the head.[75]

The officers and the commission maintained that they were within their authority to defend themselves. They claimed that they "were shot at and returned seven shots in reply." But the commonwealth's attorney and the citizens of Franklin and Patrick Counties disagreed. They believed that the officers had acted with malice and murdered Thomas.[76]

In August 1920, the officers were indicted and tried for the murder of Thomas, but after much deliberation, the jury acquitted them. The prohibition commission and its officers celebrated the decision, believing it to be "a great victory for the government and is taken to mean that bootleggers can be shot down if they fail to halt when called upon to do so." Folks in the mountains of Franklin and Patrick Counties were none too happy with the

Downtown Rocky Mount during the era of Prohibition. *Courtesy of the Town of Rocky Mount.*

verdict, so much so, that the *Richmond Dispatch* reported that "powder would be burning in the two counties."[77]

Peters and Brame's aggressive strategy also did not sit well with the business community, politicians or citizens, for that matter. Many saw the killing of Posey Thomas, and the seizure and embargo of meal, yeast and copper, as overreach. The commission had already angered the railroads that operated in the state. On several occasions, agents had harassed passengers and waylaid trains as they searched rail cars for illegal liquor. There was a public outcry, and the governor and members of the General Assembly dismissed Peters, reduced the commission's budget and directed it to take a less zealous approach in its enforcement of prohibition laws.[78]

The commission's effort to stop whiskey making in Franklin County was doomed from the start. Moonshiners in the county had successfully eluded and fought off revenue officers for well over one hundred years. And with local authorities and citizens unwilling to cooperate with agents, there was little interruption in the business of making and running bootleg liquor.

Even those outside Franklin County applauded the county's resistance to Prohibition. In a 1932 editorial with the headline "Franklin, There She Stands," the *Times Dispatch* celebrated the county's "unique distinction among those communities of Virginia which laugh at so-called moral gestures and

The Franklin County Court House was something of a revolving door during the 1920s and '30s. Bootleggers came in, and they came out. But most, however, received little more than a slap on the wrist. Everyone, it seemed, including the sheriff and the commonwealth's attorney, believed that moonshiners should be left alone. *Courtesy of V.P.I. and S.U. Special Collections.*

harry hapless dry agents." The challenge to enforcing Prohibition in Franklin County, noted the *Dispatch*, was monumental:

> *Agents say that not only are the moonshiners themselves as foxy as the foxiest, but in Franklin County there is, for prohibition purposes, an exasperating spirit of clannishness. Neighbor watches over neighbor. Devices for mountain communication would do credit to the signal corps of an army.*[79]

The authors believed that one "must admire ingeniousness wherever found." The "moonshiner in this picturesque section of Virginia regards himself as being quite in the class with the fellow who makes the better mousetrap and forces the world to his door, though it be in a wilderness."[80]

Even when they were successful in catching moonshiners, judges and grand juries were reluctant to indict those who had been arrested. Such was the case of a bootlegger who was caught "red-handed" in June 1920. Despite evidence for a "perfect case," said authorities, the grand jury in Roanoke did not indict or "pay any heed to the work of the officers." Chief Brame complained that "there was a lack of cooperation on the part of some judges of the circuit courts in upholding the law....He described them as 'weaklings.'"[81]

~ ~ ~ ~ ~ ~ ~

PROHIBITION OFFICERS WERE ALSO at a disadvantage in that moonshiners employed the latest advances in communication, surveillance and transportation. Though rare in mountain communities in the 1920s and 1930s, telephones enabled people in some areas of the county to alert still operators of the approach of Prohibition officers. A more common and effective way to spot the authorities, however, was to hire scouts equipped with field glasses. Perched on mountaintops, they could easily alert moonshiners with a rifle shot, a bell or a horn used for calling dogs.[82]

With the mass production of automobiles by the mid-1920s, moonshiners had access to a more efficient and speedy way to get whiskey to cities such as Roanoke, Danville, Winston-Salem and Greensboro. State and local authorities, of course, also used automobiles to stop the flow of illegal liquor, but they were no match for the skilled drivers and mechanics that moonshiners employed to run their product and maintain their vehicles.

Bootlegger mechanics and drivers, for example, came up with a multitude of techniques to improve the performance of their vehicles and avoid capture. Improvements in carburetors, gear ratios and the introduction of Ford's V-8 in 1932 enabled drivers to outrun pursuing Prohibition and revenue officers who, for a lack of funding, often had underpowered vehicles. Metal wheel skirts were added to prevent officers from shooting out tires. And reinforced suspensions were installed so that a driver could carry hundreds of gallons of whiskey without riding low and arousing suspicion. These measures, together with the tactic of using a pilot or blockade car to prevent officers from overtaking those vehicles that were actually carrying liquor, were particularly frustrating for authorities.[83]

One Franklin County liquor runner and blockade driver who won national fame during the 1920s and '30s was Willie Carter Sharpe. Although Sharpe had served time at the Federal Women's Prison in West Virginia, her dark hair and diamond-studded teeth made her something

Opposite, top: The Ford V-8 became the vehicle of choice for whiskey haulers, especially the 1940 Ford Deluxe being towed here by ATF and ABC agents. *Courtesy of Morris Stephenson.*

Opposite, bottom: Car engines were modified in the 1930s and '40s with additional two-barrel carburetors for quick acceleration and overall speed for eluding revenue agents. *Courtesy of Morris Stephenson.*

Right: The writer Sherwood Anderson became fascinated with Willie Carter Sharpe during the 1935 Conspiracy Trial and modeled the main character of his 1936 novel, *Kit Brandon*, after her. *Courtesy of Encyclopedia Virginia.*

of an exotic heroine to the people of the mountains. Skilled at negotiating the torturous roads in Shooting Creek and Runnett Bag at high speeds, she managed to haul close to 110 gallons of whiskey into Roanoke every day during her career as a runner.[84]

But her true notoriety came from her exploits as a driver of the block car. Described by the *Richmond Dispatch* as "Franklin's Outlaw Heroine," Sharpe was noted for outwitting "pursuing officers by blocking their attempts to reach the liquor cars ahead, or to lead them off the trail in a mad dash over circuitous side roads while the main caravan continued to its destination."[85]

The writer Sherwood Anderson found Willie to be both an attractive and compelling woman. When she and forty-five others were indicted in 1935 for their role in a conspiracy in Franklin County between local authorities and moonshiners, he attended the trial and wrote a short article in *Liberty Magazine* about her career as a rumrunner. Willie, reported Anderson, had a "passion for automobiles and developed into a fast and efficient driver." A local businessman who admired her skill, said Anderson, "saw her go right through the main street of our town and there was a federal car after her. They were banging away, trying to shoot down her tires, and she was driving 75 miles an hour." Much to the man's delight, Willie got away.[86]

Fascinated by her courage and her willingness to flout convention, Anderson modeled the main character of his 1936 novel, *Kit Brandon*, after her. Like Willie, Kit is a young girl who longs to escape the isolation and primitiveness of the southern mountains. And again, like Willie, her life dramatically changes when she moves to the city and joins up with a gang of big-time bootleggers.[87]

While Willie's adventures would come to an end with her indictment in the 1935 conspiracy trial, thanks to Anderson and local newspapers, her singular feats as a whiskey hauler would live on in literature and in regional and national folklore. Interestingly, she would even become known abroad. Today, there is a cocktail bar named for her in the French Mediterranean city of Montpellier.

~ ~ ~ ~ ~ ~ ~

BOTH DURING PROHIBITION AND after, bootleggers in Franklin County came up with every ruse possible to disguise their operations. Believing that officers would be reluctant to search places of worship, some situated their stills on church grounds or in some cases inside the church. Others found cemeteries to be a resourceful way to conceal stills and stores of whiskey. One group of bootleggers in 1917 decided to even enlist the services of the dead to hide a barrel of whiskey:

> *Prohibition officers have discovered a new trick on the part of moonshiners in Franklin County. They opened a grave near a public road and put a barrel of whiskey on top of the occupant. A pump was placed in the barrel and the liquor was taken out as orders were received.*[88]

While the officers "stood guard and finally captured a number of men," they found that the "liquor had been almost entirely consumed."[89]

Sixty years later, in 1979, a number of moonshiners came up with a similarly ingenious way to use a cemetery to camouflage their distilling operations. In the Henry section of the county, agents spied what at first glance appeared to be a family graveyard located on top of a hill. But as they approached the spot, they saw that the tombstones were actually stacks of cinderblocks painted white. To add to the deception, the moonshiners had decorated each marker with plastic flowers. Near the "cemetery," they discovered a still place with electricity from a nearby abandoned house. Inside they found eighteen 1,800-gallon stills capable of producing 2,000 gallons of whiskey a week.[90]

During the 1940s, the back seat of the Ford V-8 Deluxe Coupe could be easily removed for extra space to haul jugs and Mason jars of whiskey. *Courtesy of Morris Stephenson.*

Ralph D. Hale and brothers David, Roger, William and Randy Philpott were arrested and indicted for making illegal whiskey at the "Cemetery Still." The U.S. Attorney's Office maintained that "they were the masterminds behind a multi-state moonshine operation at the fake cemetery." A federal judge imposed fines on the men as high as $10,000. Each also received prison sentences.[91]

Moonshiners painted cinderblocks white and arranged plastic flowers around them to disguise their nearby operation as part of a cemetery. *Courtesy of Morris Stephenson.*

The Philpotts were the sons of Jaybird Philpott and had been introduced to whiskey making at an early age. Jaybird had made and run moonshine for much of his life. And like most bootleggers in Franklin County, he had had, on more than one occasion, run-ins with revenue agents. They were continuing a tradition and a business that provided them with a steady, albeit risky, source of income.

But making and running whiskey had an allure that went beyond the money it put in men's and women's pockets. Willie Carter Sharpe told writer Sherwood Anderson, who was covering the conspiracy trial for *Liberty Magazine*, that it "was the excitement that got [her]" and that most of those who ran whiskey "were mostly kids who liked the excitement." In the same

A fresh-cut tree was placed in a pipe in the ground to hide the entrance to the path to a still place. *Courtesy of Morris Stephenson.*

article, Willie recalled that a number of women who "had in their veins what you call the best blood in Virginia" asked to go along with her on a whiskey run. These ladies, said Willie, "wanted the kick of it."[92]

Young men, in particular, were drawn to the thrill of defying the law and outfoxing Prohibition or revenue officers. Writing in *One Hundred Proof*, onetime moonshiner Henry Law explained in an honest and compelling story the exhilaration he got from eluding the authorities in Franklin County. After he saw revenue agents approach his still in Ferrum, Henry quickly climbed a hill above the still site. With an officer chasing him, he then ran across an open field, jumped a ditch, crossed the main road and slipped out of sight into the woods. It was a close call, but he had gotten away:

After I heard the sound of his boots, I then heard him gasp for what sounded like his last breath. That's how close we were to each other, and believe me, it took all that I had to keep him from hearing my breaths. But I knew it was over; he didn't have anything for me. After catching his breath, he headed back toward the still place. I threw up every bit of the big breakfast Mom fed us before leaving Dad's that morning. Now that's what I've been telling ya'll! What a rush! I loved it.[93]

Henry learned the craft of making liquor and how to avoid getting caught from his father, Amos Law, and kinfolk. Amos made and ran liquor most of his life, and Henry admired him for his courage and his willingness to take chances and live a bit outside the law. "I feel for all people who are satisfied with a mundane life that is always safe and predictable," wrote Henry. "I don't think a man has truly lived," he asserted, "until he has pushed the limits of the law, taken that risk and felt that rush consuming his entire body." His father had done just that. "When I look at my Dad's life," he concluded, "I know for a fact that he has lived, felt that rush, and pushed the envelope to the limit."[94]

Like Henry and his father, longtime Franklin County bootlegger Frank Mills enjoyed the thrill of tricking or outwitting revenue agents and, of course, the profit. But there was something else that drew him to making whiskey. Late one night while tending his still, he came to understand just why he was a moonshiner:

As I sat there on a box and listened to the night sounds, the moonlight filtered through the trees. The fire was popping and sizzling like only an open fire can do. The golden flame put a soft light around the still place. The moonlight sparkled [in] a half gallon of moonshine that sat on a full case.[95]

Despite the fear of getting caught, there was a certain beauty and peace that came to him in the mountain woods that evening. "I knew then," he realized, "why I loved making moonshine whiskey."[96]

Chapter 4

CONSPIRACY

Deputy Jeff Richards got into his 1931 Ford Roadster on the night of October 12, 1934, in Rocky Mount and headed to Callaway to bring in Jim Smith, a Black man who was suspected of stealing clothes from a local store. Jeff was a bit perturbed. This was a minor offense, and why couldn't this wait until the morning? C. Carter Lee, the commonwealth's attorney, insisted, however, that he bring Smith in that night.[97]

He would have to make the trip alone. Edgar Beckett, his partner, said he felt sick and asked Jeff to drive him home. Known to citizens as "Mutt and Jeff," they always traveled together when policing the county. It was unusual to see Jeff engaged in official business this evening without Edgar.[98]

After picking up Smith, Jeff began the trip back to Rocky Mount. But just around 9:30 p.m., as he passed Antioch Church of the Brethren, a car pulled in behind him. Suddenly, a shotgun blast shattered the rear window. Another shot hit him in the back. Despite his injury, Jeff managed to stop the car in the road and get out. Smith, who was in the back seat, also got out and began to run. Jeff pulled his gun, but almost immediately another round of shots from a .45-caliber pistol and a twelve-gauge shotgun hit him.[99]

Investigating officers found Richards's Roadster with its lights on, in gear and the switch on. Richards and Smith were discovered in the road. Jeff was lying facedown, fifteen feet to the rear of his vehicle, with fifteen rounds of bullets and buckshot in his body, one of which was fired point-

Deputy Jeff Richards, at the time of his assassination, was known as the collector and treasurer of the "granny fees" moonshiners paid to make and haul their whiskey in Franklin County. *Courtesy of T. Keister Greer.*

blank directly into his head. Smith, who lay in the front of the car, had been felled, like Richards, by buckshot from a twelve-gauge shotgun. The car itself, reported the *Roanoke Times*, "was riddled with bullets.... There are thirteen dents made by the shot in the rear part of the car body, 12 holes through the top, and 24 holes in the windshield."[100]

The killing of Richards attracted headlines all over the state and set tongues wagging in the county. Richards was one of many defendants about to testify in what came to be known as the "Great Moonshine Conspiracy." The conspiracy, said federal investigators, occurred during the years between 1928 and 1933 and consisted of a scheme hatched by the commonwealth's attorney, county law enforcement, moonshiners and even a business to defraud the federal government of tax money. It was the testimony of witnesses directly connected to the conspiracy that led

Both Deputies Charlie Rakes (*left*) and Jeff Richards received cash payments from moonshiners. Like Richards, Rakes never testified at the 1935 Conspiracy Trial. He died of pneumonia two weeks before Richards's murder in 1934. *Courtesy of T. Keister Greer.*

the grand jury indictment and subsequent trial in Harrisonburg.[101]

C. Carter Lee, the grandnephew of Robert E. Lee; Sheriff Pete Hodges; and his son Wilson, who succeeded him, said the indictment, allowed moonshiners to operate as long as they paid a fee. Witnesses testified in the trial that moonshiners would have to pay ten dollars to transport a load of whiskey and fifty dollars per month to operate a still. Those who paid their monthly fees were encouraged to break up the stills of moonshiners who refused to pay up. Deputy T. Jefferson "Jeff" Richards collected and kept track of these "Granny Fees" on a regular basis. Richards was also the liaison between moonshiners and the Ferrum Mercantile Company, which provided still operators with yeast, malt, sugar, copper tubing and other supplies.[102]

Commonwealth's Attorney C. Carter Lee, grandnephew of Robert E. Lee, was indicted as both the originator and key benefactor of the "Granny Fee" payment system in the 1935 Conspiracy Trial. *Courtesy of T. Keister Greer.*

~ ~ ~ ~ ~ ~ ~

As ONE OF THOSE indicted, Jeff Richards, given his direct role in the conspiracy, would, no doubt, go to prison, and so would his partner Edgar Beckett. But Jeff had let it be known that he was not going to take the fall for the higher-ups who had concocted the scheme. For a possible reduction in his sentence, he was going to name names. He recognized, however, that his decision to testify for the prosecution put him in danger of being murdered. He even told people that he was not long for this world.[103]

There is little doubt that Richards's impending testimony cost him his life and the life of Jim Smith. But who was responsible? Some suspected that Lee, who was believed to be the kingpin of the operation, had ordered the killing. Yet there may have been others, including his fellow officers and even his partner Edgar Beckett, who wanted him dead. Despite the fact that Richards's killing was more than likely connected to the conspiracy trial, the federal prosecutor decided to focus his efforts on the conspiracy between moonshiners and Lee to defraud the federal government. The investigation into Richards's murder would have to wait.

Forrest Bondurant, whose father, T.G. Bondurant, was a county supervisor, became one of the government's most important witnesses. Before a grand jury, he testified that in 1928, he had asked Deputy Sheriff Henry Abshire to make arrangements with Jeff Richards and Edgar Beckett to allow him and his brothers to make and haul their whiskey uninterrupted in the county. According to Forrest, he paid Abshire twenty-five to thirty dollars during the months they were making whiskey.[104]

Forrest further exposed the extent of the Franklin County Sheriff's Department's corruption and abuse of authority when he was asked about his and his brother Jack's confrontation with Deputies Charlie Rakes and Henry Abshire on December 20, 1930. According to Forrest, the two officers had set up a blockade at Maggodee Creek Bridge on what is today Route 122 from Rocky Mount to Bedford. Rakes and Abshire told him and his brother that they could not pass unless they surrendered one of their cars containing 150 gallons of liquor. Jack believed that he had earlier paid the requisite "Granny Fee" but offered Rakes seventy-five dollars anyway.[105]

Rakes was not familiar with Jack or Forrest and refused the money. Unwilling to give up their liquor, Jack grabbed the keys from the car. It was then that Charlie Rakes, said Forrest, opened fire, hitting Jack in the left shoulder. Forrest, who at the time was scuffling with Henry Abshire, broke free and ran to his brother. But before he had taken four or five steps, Rakes shot him through the abdomen.[106]

Jack's and Forrest's wounds were so serious that they were taken to Lewis-Gale Hospital in Roanoke. The bullet that struck Jack's left shoulder careened through his lungs and passed into his right arm. The bullet that hit Forrest traveled through his stomach and lodged in his spine, causing paralysis in his right leg. After several weeks in the hospital and blood transfusions, both brothers made a full recovery from their wounds. Forrest and Jack, however, were indicted and charged with offering a bribe to an officer of the law and for transporting illegal liquor with firearms. They received suspended two-year sentences.[107]

Charlie Rakes claimed, without evidence, that he fired his pistol only after the brothers drew their guns. Although he was indicted for the felonious wounding of Jack and Forrest, he was never formally charged. In February 1931, he resigned as deputy sheriff. He was later considered to be a valuable witness for the government in the Conspiracy Trial but died of pneumonia in 1934, only a couple of weeks before Richards and his prisoner's murder.[108]

The Great Moonshine Conspiracy Trial resulted in thirty-one people, along with the Ferrum Mercantile Company, being convicted for conspiracy to defraud the government. Significantly, C. Carter Lee was not among them. Lee's attorneys had maintained that the "Granny Fees" were simply fines that he imposed on moonshiners for breaking the law—even though no other commonwealth's attorney in the state used such a practice. The jury, however, was not fooled. All the jurors, with the exception of Edgar Marshall, were convinced of Lee's guilt. Marshall, however, insisted that Lee was not guilty and refused to listen to all reason and evidence to the contrary. As a consequence, the jury had no choice but to acquit Lee.[109]

The foreman, as well as other members of the jury, found Marshall's behavior suspicious and said so in depositions that led to a series of federal indictments and a second trial in Harrisonburg in 1936. This time, a jury would have to determine if the twenty-four men named in the indictments were guilty of jury tampering in the moonshine conspiracy trial. In a strange turn of events, C. Carter Lee, who perhaps bribed Marshall and others, was not indicted and would be called as a witness for the prosecution. Thirteen of those charged pled guilty and received probation. The others who pleaded not guilty received harsher sentences—both fines and imprisonment. Lee emerged from the proceedings unscathed and would go on to serve as Franklin County's commonwealth's attorney until 1943.[110]

~ ~ ~ ~ ~ ~ ~

BUT WHAT ABOUT JEFF Richards? His murder and that of Jim Smith were still unsolved. After almost two years, investigators and Carter Lee decided that there was enough evidence to indict Paul and Hubbard Duling, two brothers who frequently ran moonshine from Franklin County to where they lived in West Virginia, for the killings.

The brothers maintained that they were innocent. But the prosecution, headed by, ironically, C. Carter Lee contended that the Dulings killed Richards in retaliation for the death of their older brother Frank. Frank, who was hauling liquor a few days before Christmas in 1933, died attempting to escape from his moving car after being chased by Franklin County and Roanoke deputies, one of whom happened to be Richards. Lee argued that the brothers believed that Richards and other officers beat Frank to death.[111]

Lee said the weapon used and the circumstances in which they were killed were similar to that of the murder of Roanoke deputy sheriff C.E. "Big Boy" Simmons. In the early morning of July 17, 1936, Simmons and his partner Charles E. Boone were driving along Route 220 between Rocky Mount and Roanoke when a car suddenly appeared in their rear-view mirror near Boones Mill. Soon after, a shotgun blast from the car hit Simmons. Boone,

Roanoke deputy sheriff C.E. "Big Boy" Simmons was assassinated in the early morning of July 17, 1936, as he and his partner Charles Boone drove along Route 220 between Rocky Mount and Roanoke. *Courtesy of Officer Down Memorial Page.*

who had been slumped in the front passenger seat sleeping, was not hit and managed to gain control of the vehicle. Simmons, however, had taken the full load of buckshot from the shotgun and died at the scene.[112]

The investigation that followed revealed that Tom Thomas, owner of Tom's Barbecue in Roanoke, had seen a car with West Virginia plates at his restaurant. After further questioning, Thomas revealed that the men in the car were Paul and Hubbard Duling. The Duling brothers, who regularly transported Franklin County liquor to West Virginia, were well known to the authorities. Their brother Frank had long been the kingpin behind the bootleg trade in West Virginia during Prohibition. Using biplanes and "souped-up" automobiles, he moved thousands of gallons of liquor out of Virginia and into West Virginia counties and towns.[113]

Frank's days of running liquor, however, came to an end one evening before Christmas in 1933. Having not gotten permission to move liquor through Franklin County, officers gave chase and shot out one of his tires. Frank jumped from the car but landed wrong on the frozen ground and broke his neck.[114]

The Duling family did not believe the official report of his death. They were convinced that Simmons and Richards, two of the officers who chased Frank, had beaten him to death. This, maintained detectives, was perhaps the motive for the murder of both Richards and Simmons.[115]

Despite scant evidence and the testimony of friends and family members that they were in West Virginia at the time, the Duling brothers were arrested for the murders and held in the Beckley jail until their extradition to Virginia. The Dulings were a tight family and were none too pleased that two of their own were being held for murders that they knew they did not commit. As the whole clan gathered in Beckley, rumors spread that they were going to spring the brothers from jail. In response, local authorities brought in extra deputies to escort Paul and Hubbard to the Virginia state line.[116]

Since the Dulings were arrested for multistate crimes, their trial was held at the federal courthouse in Roanoke. The prosecuting attorney, Frank

Tavenner Jr., based his case on witnesses' testimony and circumstantial evidence, albeit flimsy, that the brothers had killed Simmons in retaliation for Frank's death. One witness, Rolla Smoot, a former sister-in-law of Frank, said she was with Paul and Hubbard in Roanoke shortly after Frank's death. According to Rolla, both brothers said that their brother would never rest until Simmons was killed on the same road as Frank.[117]

B.A. Davis, the defense attorney, maintained that the killing of Simmons, as well as that of Richards, stemmed from a conspiracy to keep both men from testifying against their fellow officers and the commonwealth's attorney. "It is a 'peculiar coincidence,'" said Davis, "that Jeff Richards should have been slain just a few days before he was expected to go before a federal grand jury and tell what he knew about the liquor conspiracy."[118] Moreover, the prosecution had no evidence, placing them physically at the spot where the murder occurred. In fact, numerous witnesses testified that they were either with the brothers or saw them on the days of the killings.[119]

After days of deliberation, the jury remained unable to reach a verdict of murder in the first degree. In an effort to salvage the government's case, Tavenner asked for a second trial; this time, he argued for the brothers to be convicted of manslaughter. The jury agreed and returned a verdict of guilty. Paul and Hubbard each received twenty years in the state penitentiary. They had just begun serving that sentence when they were indicted in 1937 for the murder of Richards and Smith.[120]

The Duling brothers' trial for the Richards murder did not go smoothly. Lawyers could not agree on a jury, and when they did, jurymen failed to reach a verdict. Eventually, the brothers were tried before a jury in Halifax County, an area where both the prosecution and the defense lawyers thought they might find an impartial jury. After eight days, Lee was able to get a verdict of guilty of murder in the first degree and a sentence of ninety-nine years for each of the brothers. The judge, however, reduced the sentence to thirty years.[121]

The Duling brothers would only serve ten years of that sentence. In 1942, Hallie Bowles, a Franklin County native who was serving in the U.S. Army in Washington State, confessed to the murders in suicide notes that he addressed to Carter Lee. The Duling brothers, said Bowles, had nothing to do with the killings. Although divorced from Bowles at the time of his suicide, Annie Bowles Snead confirmed in an affidavit that Bowles was one of the killers:

During the month of December 1936, my husband Hallie Bowles took me in an automobile to the spot where Jeff Richards and Jim Smith were killed. He told me that he and one [other] *person killed these people. He showed me a handkerchief tied on a post at or near the spot where Jeff Richards was killed, and showed me the pine tree by which he was standing when he fired the shots.*[122]

Bowles made it clear to her that if she "ever told this to anyone that he would kill me."[123]

Bowles would also tell Howard Greene, a friend of his who lived in Callaway, that he was one of the assassins. In an affidavit given in October 1943, Greene stated that he saw Bowles quite often. In fact, one day less than two months following the murders, Greene saw that Bowles had a considerable sum of money on him. Recognizing that Greene might be curious as to why he had so much cash, Bowles, said Greene, then told him that he was paid to kill Richards and Smith and that he must promise to never tell anyone.[124]

The man believed to be Bowles's accomplice, Sherman Wimmer, never confessed. But Wimmer's common-law wife, Viola Manning, signed an affidavit while he was serving time in the state penitentiary for an unrelated crime attesting to the fact that she believed he was one of the killers. According to Viola, "Sherman Wimmer made remarks to me from time to time, over a period of three years, that convinced me that he was involved in the killing of Jeff Richards."[125]

After he learned that Bowles had left suicide notes admitting to the crime, said Viola, he became paranoid and erratic:

He kept his gun loaded all the time and seemed to think somebody was coming after him all the time. Every time a strange automobile would pass up and down the road he would run out the back and tell me to tell the people that Sherman Wimmer did not stay there, and that I knew nothing about him.[126]

Viola's affidavit suggests that it was not the authorities that Wimmer feared. On the contrary, he perhaps believed that the person or persons who paid him and Bowles to kill Richards would now want to eliminate him since Bowles had indicated that he had a partner in the crime. In 1944, the Duling brothers' lawyers presented the suicide notes and the affidavits to Frank Tavenner, who had prosecuted the case. They also explained that new evidence indicated that the weapon used in the crime—a high-powered twelve-gauge pump shotgun that belonged to the Dulings—had been loaned to a deputy sheriff and others in the county for hunting deer and other big game at the time. This meant that the shotgun could have easily gotten into the hands of the actual killers. Eventually, both Paul and Hubbard would be paroled by 1949. They returned to West Virginia and lived out their last days still insisting that they were innocent.[127]

~ ~ ~ ~ ~ ~ ~

THE GREAT MOONSHINE CONSPIRACY left many casualties in its wake. Jeff Richards, Jim Smith, Clarence E. Simmons and Hallie Bowles were dead, and the Duling brothers served time in prison for murders they did not commit. Men's reputations were also sullied and trust in the integrity of law enforcement diminished. Some found the humiliation of getting caught up in the conspiracy and the attempt to bribe jurors unbearable.

On April 3, 1936, S. Claude Slusher, a prominent farmer and livestock breeder, who was one of twenty-four men indicted for jury tampering, grabbed his shotgun and went to the barn on a farm he owned near Willis in Floyd County. After leaving a note on the door explaining where his farmhands could find him, he went to a nearby abandoned house. Inside, he sat on the floor with the muzzle of his shotgun gun aimed at his chest. Using a stick, he managed to press the trigger and fire the weapon. The blast killed him instantly.[128]

Chapter 5

THUNDER IN THE MOUNTAINS

On a March evening in 1950, Alcohol Beverage Control officer William Wayland retired to his home in Rocky Mount after a long day of tracking down stills and moonshiners in the Franklin County mountains. Exhausted from the day's activities, he finally turned in around midnight. Around 3:00 a.m., however, he was awakened by a loud boom and the sound of shattering glass. As he ran outside, he could see smoke enveloping his automobile. As he would later learn, someone had exploded five sticks of dynamite under his car. The explosion did minimal damage to his vehicle, but it did blow out the front windows of the Wayland home.[129]

The men who set the charge apparently did not intend to kill him or his family members, but they clearly aimed to intimidate him into desisting from his aggressive hunt for and prosecution of the county's bootleggers. Wayland's wife and children were frightened by the blast, but he was not. On the contrary, he planned "to keep up his work of still busting," said an article in the *Clifton Forge Gazette*, "until he runs out of stills."[130]

In the weeks following the explosion, Wayland and his fellow ABC officers made good on his vow to keep busting stills in Franklin County. In March alone, 29 of the 129 stills destroyed in Virginia were found in what officials described as the "hotbed of bootlegging in the state." By the end of the year, officers had conducted 352 raids and seized 173 illegal stills in the county. The message was clear. Any attempt to intimidate revenue officers would be met with rigorous enforcement of the law.[131]

~ ~ ~ ~ ~ ~ ~

SUCH ATTACKS ON REVENUE agents, however, were actually rare in Franklin County. While it is true that there had been open warfare between moonshiners and federal and state revenue officers who ventured into Runnett Bag, Endicott and Shooting Creek during the late nineteenth century, those confrontations were largely seen as mountain communities defending their way of life against outsiders.

Yet by the 1930s, attitudes toward revenuers had changed. Many law-abiding men in the county who had never made liquor needed jobs and found employment as revenue officers. Since many of these men were born and raised in the area and perhaps even friends with moonshiners and their families, it was understood among mountain folk that you did not shoot them if they happened to raid your still. They were sworn to uphold the law, and if they caught you, it was just your misfortune.[132]

But there was a notable exception to this code. Raymond Sloan, who worked for the Works Progress Administration as a gatherer of mountain folklore during the 1930s, explained in a 1979 interview that "if their neighbor friends, a man in the community decided to join up with the revenue force after he had bought and sold liquor all his life, he was a turncoat and that was the man who got shot." Sloan's family knew this all too well. Homer Boyd, his wife's uncle, made whiskey both before and after his service in World War I. But during the 1920s, he took a job as a Prohibition officer in the county. His employment didn't last long; he was killed in an ambush.[133]

For most of the men who had not violated this mountain code, there were relatively safe and secure jobs in the county as ABC officers. After the repeal of both the Eighteenth Amendment and the statute that banned alcohol in Virginia, the General Assembly passed legislation setting up in 1934 the Department of Alcohol Beverage Control. Virginians who wished to purchase hard spirits now had to buy them from an ABC store. Businesses wishing to sell beer or wine would have to purchase licenses from the department. The General Assembly eventually expanded the powers of the department in 1936, giving designated ABC officers full police power to assist local and federal authorities in the enforcement of the laws against bootlegging.[134]

With the availability of good-quality liquor at ABC stores and a state police force specifically charged with finding and destroying bootlegging operations, there was a decline in illegal distilling in the Commonwealth. T.K. Sexton, who served as the head of the ABC inspection division, reported in 1936 that figures from actual seizures of illegal liquor and mash indicated that "there is at the present time not more than one-third or one-fourth of the moonshining and bootlegging that there was in Virginia during the last years of prohibition."[135]

No doubt the state's new campaign against untaxed liquor convinced some Franklin County moonshiners that it was time to end their operations. But tradition and profit had their allure, and men in the western sections of the county kept making liquor well into the 1980s. And despite the fact that whiskey could be purchased in government stores and private businesses around the country, they knew that there was still a strong demand in bars and shot houses, particularly in the northeastern United States, for well-crafted 90 to 100 proof mountain whiskey.

This demand kept both moonshiners and ABC agents busy throughout the 1950s. According to figures released by the ABC Board, there were 339 raids and 157 stills seized in 1952 in Franklin County—more than double that of any of the other one hundred counties in Virginia. By the end of the 1970s, the county remained the number-one producer of illegal whiskey in the state, maybe even the nation. As a consequence, it was the only county with four full-time ABC agents assigned to keep check on illegal distilling.[136]

For nearly thirty years, Agents J.A. (Jim) Bowman, V.K. (Ken) Stoneman, Jack A. Powell and John A. Hix labored day in, day out trying to stem the flow of moonshine in what was coming to be known as the Moonshine Capital of the World. The work was strenuous. Moonshiners during the 1950s and early '60s located their operations far from the road and used horses and sleds to transport equipment and their finished product to and from the still site. Often hiking deep into the hills and hollows of Endicott, Ferrum, Callaway, Shooting Creek, Henry and Runnett Bag, the four men spent long hours breaking up still operations and seizing thousands of gallons of mash and whiskey. It was not unusual for the team to find and destroy as many as four or five stills a day.[137]

Bowman, Stoneman, Powell and Hix, however, were under no illusions. Whiskey making was ingrained in the culture of the county's people. John M. Wright, the director of enforcement for the ABC Commission, explained why Franklin County consistently ranked among the top-ten illicit liquor-making counties in the nation. "They have isolation, rugged terrain, lots of good water and a family tradition down there," said Wright. "There are folks in Franklin," he observed, "whose fathers and grandfathers were moonshiners and they are, too."[138]

Above: ABC agents worked tirelessly to stop the flow of illegal liquor in the county. *Courtesy of Morris Stephenson.*

Opposite: The Hub Restaurant in Rocky Mount opened in the 1930s and became a popular dining spot for ABC agents, local law enforcement and bootleggers. *Courtesy of the Town of Rocky Mount.*

Jim Bowman agreed. The tradition was so strong and the money so appealing that those who got caught would quickly return to making whiskey after paying their fines or serving time in jail. "It was just like a recycling process," said Bowman in a 1981 interview following his retirement. "The ones you sent up in November," he commented, "they'd be back and you'd try them in May." Bowman and his fellow agents caught one moonshiner five times between scheduled court dates. "They can keep it under control," concluded Bowman, "but I don't believe they will ever stop it." Virginia, he mused, was "fortunate that there's not but one Franklin County."[139]

Agents Bowman, Stoneman, Powell and Hix did their best to not only find illegal stills but also render them useless in the future to bootleggers. Using heavy axes, agents split open cookers and broke apart mash boxes. But they soon learned that moonshiners were quite adept at salvaging parts and patching their stills. And given the fact that operators were now constructing eight-hundred-gallon submarine-type stills, ABC agents needed a more efficient and effective way to make sure still parts were not reusable.

Eventually, agents found a solution to the problem. Wherever possible, they would dynamite still operations. Beginning in the early 1960s, Agents Bowman, Stoneman and Hix routinely kept two cases of dynamite in their Jeep whenever hunting stills in the county. The use of such high explosives, of course, was dangerous. If not careful, they could set an entire mountain on fire or get killed or seriously injured.

Newspaper reporter Morris Stephenson frequently accompanied the three agents on major still busts in Franklin County. Taking pictures and recording the details of each bust, he witnessed the destruction of some of the largest stills in the state's history. In *A Night of Makin Likker*, his memoir about his years covering both the legal and illegal side of moonshining in the county,

This page: ABC agents began using dynamite to destroy still operations during the 1950s. *Courtesy of Morris Stephenson.*

Opposite: Just below this hillside Jaybird Philpott located his steam still operation. *Courtesy of Morris Stephenson.*

Stephenson recalls how close he came to getting killed while photographing the dynamiting of a still belonging to Jaybird Philpott in Henry:

> *They unloaded the explosives and quickly carried them to the base of the hill.... When finished, they ran the electrical wire about halfway up the hill and connected it to a detonation box. The t-shaped handle was up. They checked to make sure I was ready to get the explosion photo.... "Fire in the hole," yelled one of the agents from Roanoke. He pushed down on the t-shaped handle....A "bam" magnified to a clap of thunder, sounded and crushed the silence. The earth vibrated under my feet as it always did.... Something quickly caught my eye. It was a large piece of galvanized metal flip-flopping its way back to earth.*[140]

The opening to Jaybird's underground still. *Courtesy of Morris Stephenson.*

The metal sheet, described Stephenson, was like a "potential guillotine," and if he didn't run back up the hill he would be its hapless victim. Luckily, he escaped unharmed, albeit a bit shaken.[141]

Stephenson actually witnessed the destruction of the largest bootlegging operation in the county's history. On December 18, 1972, Virginia Alcohol Beverage Control officers Jim Bowman and Ken Stoneman, together with federal Alcohol Tobacco and Firearms agents Bob Bodine and Ken Kraig, grabbed their heavy axes and began the hard work of destroying the twenty-four eight-hundred-gallon submarine stills they had found just four miles southwest of Ferrum. The largest in the state's history to date, this outfit was similar to the twenty eight-hundred-gallon operations they had broken up in February in roughly the same area. The county now held the

Morris Stephenson photographed the destruction of the still place that was disguised as a cemetery. *Courtesy of Morris Stephenson.*

record for the number, size and capacity of stills found and destroyed in Virginia for the year.[142]

Submarine or blackpot stills were becoming the most common way to distill illegal liquor in the county by the 1970s. Low to the ground with wooden sides and curved, metal ends, these large stills were capable of producing thousands of gallons of whiskey in a short amount of time. They were also less expensive to make. Instead of using the more expensive and preferred copper of earlier years, moonshiners were fashioning their stills out of scrap metal and using car radiators instead of copper worms in the condensation process.[143]

But it was not just these high-capacity, inexpensive stills that allowed moonshiners to turn out greater quantity. Unlike in the past, still operators

Left: The remains of a Franklin County still after being dynamited. *Courtesy of Morris Stephenson.*

Below: The largest illegal distilling operation discovered in Franklin County consisted of twenty-four eight-hundred-gallon submarine-type stills. *Courtesy of Morris Stephenson.*

Reporter and photographer Morris Stephenson, who accompanied ABC agents on many raids on illegal distilling operations, was fascinated with the ingenuity of Franklin County moonshiners. Here he tries his hand at filling jugs with whiskey at a still site. *Courtesy of Morris Stephenson.*

were now fermenting the mash directly in the still rather than in mash boxes. This saved time and labor, but it produced an inferior grade of whiskey in the opinion of many moonshiners. Quantity over quality was now the driving force in the liquor trade. The mountaineers who once took great pride in making their product were being supplanted by money men who provided the funding for five-hundred- to eight-hundred-gallon submarine stills that churned out a whiskey that many old-timers felt was unfit to drink.

Chapter *6*

MOUNTAIN VIGILANTES

John E. Nowlin, who lived in Runnett Bag, eked out a living doing odd jobs and occasionally pilfering local farmers' property. He was also known to have earned a few dollars here and there reporting the location of whiskey stills in the area. On August 15, 1897, Thomas Spencer put out a warrant for Nowlin's arrest for stealing pickles and butter from his springhouse. Food was a precious commodity in the mountains, and people did not take such thefts lightly. After his arrest, Nowlin was taken to a local justice of peace to stand trial. While he was offered bail, he did not have the means to secure his release. Instead of taking Nowlin to the county jail in Rocky Mount, he was left in the custody of Spencer.[144]

News soon spread in the community that Nowlin had been captured and was being housed in Spencer's home. Determined to rid the county of the hated informant, a group of heavily armed men forced their way into the Spencer home on the evening of August 16. Now cornered and with no means of escape, Nowlin was shot three times in the abdomen, heart and spinal column. He died almost immediately from his wounds. Dr. John W. Simmons, who happened to be in the area on other business, performed the postmortem. Much to the chagrin of state and federal authorities, the coroner's jury ruled that Nowlin "was shot to death by unknown parties." Neither Spencer nor others in Runnett Bag were willing to identify Nowlin's killers.[145]

While most county citizens who lived in the mountains refused to inform on their neighbors, there were those who reported the location of stills or illegal whiskey to revenue agents. Why would they take such a risk given the likelihood of community censure and possibly assassination? In return for their assistance, informers often received cash payments. There were also those who might have done so as a way of settling a score with someone in the community.

But there were those too who sincerely felt that the liquor trade promoted drunkenness, violence and contempt for the law and was an impediment to the county's cultural, educational and economic development. Whatever their motives, one thing was almost certain—anyone found to have revealed the whereabouts of a still to revenue officers chanced a violent reprisal—maybe, as in John Nowlin's case, even death.

~ ~ ~ ~ ~ ~ ~

Throughout much of the South's history, men have taken the law into their own hands to protect their honor, accepted customs and values, their livelihood and their families. This was particularly true in the more remote areas of the Appalachians and Franklin County as well. Anyone, no matter their status or position, who stepped over the line or threatened, for example, the whiskey business was subject to physical harm or banishment.

This retributive system of justice had its origins in Northern Ireland and Northern Britain. There, individuals, families and extended kin maintained order along the borderlands, a region far from the lines of authority. Given the absence of sheriffs or officers of the law, people had to make their own justice. And as these settlers, largely Scots-Irish, made their way into the backcountry of Virginia and the Carolinas, they continued this tradition. Known in the Virginia Piedmont and Blue Ridge as "Lynch's law," this vigilantism became the accepted way to protect property and one's livelihood.[146]

While the exact derivation of what also came to be known as "Judge Lynch" or "Lynching" is uncertain, the phrase or term most likely came from the actions of two Virginians—William Lynch and/or Charles Lynch. William Lynch, who lived in Pittsylvania County during the late eighteenth century, had a formal agreement with his neighbors to protect the citizens of the county from lawlessness and "inflict such corporal punishment on him or them, as to us shall seem adequate to the crime committed or the damage sustained."[147] As a colonel in the Virginia militia during the Revolutionary War, Charles Lynch, in neighboring Bedford County, and his fellow officers hunted down and punished those they suspected of being Loyalists in southwestern Virginia. Notably, though not directly related, both Charles's and William Lynch's families were Scots-Irish from Northern Ireland.[148]

~ ~ ~ ~ ~ ~ ~

ACTS OF VIOLENCE IN the mountains were so common that newspapers could at times be taken in by sensational accounts of killings in the county. According to a January 1905 story entitled "Shot to Death at His Door" in the *Richmond Times Dispatch*, a gang of moonshiners murdered Henry Moore, the young ward of Captain Bill Thompson, a successful and well-respected farmer in the Dillon's Mill area of the county. As Moore was called out of his house, said the article, he was met with a volley of gunfire that killed him instantly. Even as he lay dead, his assassins, it was reported, "poured volley after volley into his prostrate body." The cause was that Moore had reputedly informed on a number of moonshiners in the area.[149]

The story of Henry Moore's murder, however, turned out to be false. Moore was very much alive. Why was the story concocted and sent to papers like the *Times Dispatch*? Was it a practical joke? Or could it have been something a bit more sinister? In other words, the story could have been intended to frighten Moore or anyone else who thought about cooperating with revenue officers.

This was the possible motive behind the gunfire that killed Doris Holcombe, a thirteen-year-old girl whose father had reportedly cooperated with revenue officers. On the afternoon of October 20, 1925, Doris ran to the window of her home in Sydnorsville to watch two men in a car pass the house. During the 1920s, automobiles were a rarity in rural, mountainous areas like Franklin County, and the sight of one often drew attention. Doris watched in amazement as the machine came into view. It was then, however, that gunshots rang out, and she fell to the floor. Doris died instantly from a bullet to her brain.[150]

Witnesses claimed that it was Roland Dix, a passenger in the car, who had fired the fatal shot. Dix was soon after arrested and charged with murder in the first degree. Although Dix and the driver of the car, Marvin Byrd, maintained that they had been drinking and that Dix fired his pistol randomly to celebrate his birthday, the commonwealth's attorney, J.P. Lee, was not convinced. He was certain that Dix had fired the shots in retaliation for Thomas Holcombe, Doris's father, reporting his still. This, together with the testimony of William Walker, who happened to be at the

Dix home following the shooting, proved, believed Lee, that the shooting was not random:

> *Walker said that Dix and Marvin Byrd came in drunk, played the Victrola for a while. During this time, Walker said, Dix confided to him that he had shot into somebody's house from the road and was afraid he had killed someone—but, the witness said Dix added, he did not care so long as he "killed the right parties."*[151]

Dix, his wife and Byrd denied that he had ever made the comments and that he had not realized what had happened until he was later arrested.

Members of the jury were faced with contradicting testimony and were taken to the scene of the crime to help them see the proximity of the house to the road. After only forty-five minutes of deliberation, the jury, much to the disappointment of Lee, returned a verdict of murder in the second degree. Like Lee, many in the Sydnorsville community remained convinced that Dix fully intended to harm someone in the Holcombe home. He received fifteen years in the state penitentiary.[152]

~ ~ ~ ~ ~ ~ ~

RUNNETT BAG WAS PROBABLY the most inhospitable place in Franklin County for anyone who provided information to state or federal authorities. It was also known as "a source of terror to revenue officers." According to newspaper reports, "several officers of the law had lost their lives while making raids, and many bitter feuds have originated from the thought that neighbor had informed against neighbor."[153]

This is why, no doubt, Frank Peters, a resident of Runnett Bag, was ambushed and killed while walking along a mountain road in September 1908. Peters was believed by many to have provided revenue officers with information regarding illicit stills in the area. Although the United States Revenue Service called for a full investigation into Peters's murder, no one was arrested or charged with the crime.[154]

Thirty-two years later, in September 1940, James Martin, a Works Progress Administration worker, was ambushed near his home in Endicott at Runnett Bag Creek. It was known to many that Martin not only had been a chief government witness in a federal moonshine conspiracy trial in 1939 but also was a paid informant for the state's Government Tax Unit.[155]

Runnett Bag Creek near Endicott was the site of much the county's moonshining operations and violence during the first half of the twentieth century. *Author's personal collection.*

Although Martin was given federal protective custody as long as he lived, his chances of surviving in Runnett Bag were slim. Stant Allen, who suspected that Martin was responsible for his arrest for operating an illegal still on his property, decided to take his revenge. On the evening of September 5, as Martin walked home from a local project, Allen killed him with a single shotgun blast to his neck. In exchange for his plea of guilty to murder in the first degree, Allen received a twenty-year sentence in the state penitentiary.[156]

~ ~ ~ ~ ~ ~ ~

THE CLERGY WERE NOT immune to the ire of moonshiners in the county. Ministers in such areas as Shooting Creek and Runnett Bag who reported whiskey making operations to revenue officers or condemned bootlegging and alcohol consumption from the pulpit were just as likely to be brutalized or killed as anyone else who dared cooperate with revenue officers. Reverend R.L. Cauley, a Baptist minister from Vinton, near Roanoke, for example, served the mountain districts of Franklin County. While riding along the Franklin County Road to his church in June 1903, he was "pulled from his horse by a party of alleged distillers who administered a terrible beating and warned him that if he returned again he would be killed."[157]

In another instance, Reverend E.V. Goad, a minister who traveled from his home in Roanoke to conduct services at several mountain churches in Franklin County, felt the wrath of local moonshiners when he dared criticize illicit liquor making. After Goad returned from church on Sunday evening, August 27, 1905, a group of county bootleggers captured the reverend at Mill Creek near Henry and demanded that the minister repeat his afternoon sermon denouncing illegal whiskey. Incensed that Goad had attacked both their livelihood and their way of life in church, they beat him senseless and then chased him out of the area. Although members of his congregation had pledged to defend the unfortunate minister, no one was willing to come to his aid.[158]

~ ~ ~ ~ ~ ~ ~

PEOPLE IN THE MOUNTAINS of Franklin County attacked and punished not only those whom they felt had betrayed them to the authorities or openly condemned whiskey making but also those whom they believed had breached or broken accepted social customs or values. In 1907, masked men visited the home of John W. Enedy and the "entire family, consisting of Enedy, his wife, mother, and wife's sister, were partially stripped and whipped with rawhides until their backs were lacerated." They were told that they were unwelcome in the community and that they must leave at once. The family was not Black, so racial hatred was not the motive. Just why they were unwelcome is uncertain.[159]

It was quite clear, however, why Richard Woods and his paramour were attacked in January 1880. Woods, a Black man, left his wife and children to live with Nancy Williams, a white woman. Williams was already ostracized in the community for bearing two illegitimate children, but now she and Woods had broken both the law and the social code prohibiting miscegenation.[160]

On the evening of January 6, a group of men forced their way into Williams's cabin in search of Woods. Finding him hiding under the cabin floor, they immediately bound him and Williams together and placed them in a wagon. After driving some distance from Williams's home, the men drew their pistols and demanded that Woods strip. Woods, however, was tied to Williams and could not fully remove his clothes. When Woods asked for assistance in unbuttoning his shirt, the leader of the party took the request as an insult and knocked him to the ground and began beating him. The other members of the party soon joined in.

Given what had happened to other men and women in the South who had committed the "unpardonable sin" of racial mixing, what transpired next was predictable:

> *The unfortunate negro, rendered desperate, at this juncture made a break from his custodians and ran but fell from exhaustion and terror before he had gone very far. He was closely pursued by the mob, who, as soon as they came up, shot him several times and killed him. Returning to the woman, she was administered a severe whipping, after which she was ordered to go home—admonished that if she did not leave the county in three days she would be hanged.*[161]

While an inquest was held the following day to investigate Wood's death, no one was ever arrested or charged for the crime.

But the violence against white and Black citizens in the county stemmed not just from fixed notions regarding race or social propriety but also fear, ignorance and superstition. Uncle "A" Finney, a ninety-year-old former slave who had belonged to George Finney before the Civil War, lived in a mountain cabin on the farm of his deceased friend and benefactor James Martin. As he was well-loved and thought harmless, white citizens both inside and outside the county were shocked to learn of his murder.[162]

On a September night in 1903, Uncle "A" was awakened by three men knocking loudly at his cabin door. When he opened the door, the men drew pistols and fired: "one shot passed entirely through the old man's head killing him instantly. Another tore away his jaw and a third passed through the neck."[163]

What harm had Uncle "A" done to the men or their families? Everyone in the community, it seemed, knew that he led a peaceful, quiet life, minding his own business and bothering no one. But according to some superstitious citizens in the mountain vicinity where he lived, Uncle "A" was a sorcerer and had placed a curse on Mrs. Mary Holley, leaving her ill and close to death. According to the *Alexandria Gazette*, it was the belief of the "ignorant people of the neighborhood" that "nothing could be done to alleviate her sufferings until the old sorcerer was murdered in his doorway."[164]

While conjuring, that is, using potions, herbs and amulets to influence events and people, has a long history in African American culture, there was no evidence that Uncle "A" actually practiced this folk art. It mattered little. Some people claimed that the death of Uncle "A" broke the spell that he had purportedly cast, and the woman regained her health.[165]

Virginia newspapers at the time were merciless in their condemnation of the murder. Many Eastern Virginia papers like the *Norfolk Landmark* and the *Daily Star* in Fredericksburg excoriated the ignorant Franklin County mountaineers who soiled the good name of Virginia:

> *If anyone in Eastern Virginia were told that a poor old negro could be murdered in cold blood within the confines of this state, without having offended man, woman or child, the person so told would smile at the imagination able to conjure up such a story, and yet this is just happened in Franklin County, this state, a few days ago. The story is pathetic enough, and enough to bring tears to the eye, and barbarous enough cruel enough to bring a blush of shame to the cheek of every Virginian.*[166]

"The reason for this act," so stated the editorial, was "the old negro, they say, was a sorcerer." Angered by the ignorance that led to the murder of Uncle "A", the author asked "if it was possible that in Virginia, enlightened by education, by religion and everything which goes to make up higher civilization, that such a belief which might not have caused surprise when the Pilgrims and Puritans first inhabited Massachusetts, can still prevail?"

The author hoped that the better people of Franklin would see to it "that the brutes who murdered the old man will meet their just reward—at the end of a rope."[167]

Chapter 7

BAD BLOOD

In 1858, Victoria Smith and James Clement came together to celebrate their wedding in lavish style. The couple were both from prominent Franklin County families, and the wedding was attended "by the elite…who flocked in large numbers, by invitation, from all parts of that section, to do honor to the joyous occasion." Victoria and James, it seemed, were headed for many years of wedded happiness and joy.[168]

But the joy was not to last. Not long into the marriage, Victoria said Clement became jealous of her continued friendship with some of her former suitors, so much so that he restricted her comings and goings and threatened violence. Eventually, Victoria became so aggrieved with her overbearing husband that she left him and initiated a suit for divorce.[169]

James Clement denied Victoria's depiction of their marriage as abusive and took exception to her assertion that he placed excessive restraints on her interaction with not only women but also other men. However, Clement did state that she should not see William Gilbert. Gilbert had been a regular guest at the Clement home—far too regular for James's liking. Gilbert, he suspected, had sought nightly assignations with Victoria. In his response to Victoria's complaint against him, he claimed that he regularly heard the doors of their home opening and shutting. He believed that on those occasions Victoria would leave their bed:

> *During the last spring or early part of summer respondent (Clement) frequently heard shaking and rapping at one of the doors this occurred about once a week, generally of a Saturday night. Sometimes when this*

> *occurred complainant (Victoria) and respondent were awake and he would*
> *look to see who it was, and occasionally he went out and around the house*
> *but could never see any one sometimes when this would happen and when*
> *the complainant thought respondent was asleep she would gently touch him*
> *to satisfy herself that he was asleep, and upon two occasions when these*
> *rappings occurred and she thought the respondent was asleep he knew her to*
> *get up and out of bed and go out of the room and remain away from fifteen*
> *minutes to half an hour.*[170]

When Clement told Victoria of his concerns, she claimed that she feared someone was trying to break into the house and that he should sleep with his pistol and Bowie knife under his pillow. James believed this was little more than a thinly veiled attempt to deflect suspicions away from her and Gilbert.[171]

James also believed that the two secretly communicated with each other by placing carefully chosen playing cards in a hollow tree near their home. This, together with the nightly opening and closing of doors, convinced him that Victoria had schemed to make him appear to be an insanely jealous husband:

> *And from circumstances and an investigation your respondent satisfied himself*
> *that the cards were sent and deposited in a particular hollow tree from whence*
> *they were taken by the said Gilbert. And while this was going on the rapping*
> *at the doors took place at night as hereinafter mentioned. Your respondent*
> *submits that under these circumstances he had just grounds for suspecting the*
> *complainant of improper intercourse with the said Gilbert. And he believes*
> *that she was either guilty or acted in the way she did for the purpose of*
> *inducing the belief on the mind of respondent that she was, in order to induce*
> *him to do or say something that might give her a pretext for carrying out her*
> *scheme of leaving him and throwing the odium of their separation on him.*[172]

Victoria denied any knowledge of the secret playing cards or any nocturnal meetings with Gilbert. James, she contended, was not only irrational but also a potentially violent husband.

It was not long after their separation that the couple and other interested parties met at Sandy Level in Pittsylvania County, where Victoria was living with her mother, for the purpose of taking depositions. Divorces during this period were granted only by the General Assembly and required depositions from the husband and wife as well as friends and family members. The meeting did not go well:

> *Here a charge was made by the husband, Mr. James Clement, which involved alike the honor of his wife and that of Mr. William P. Gilbert, a young gentleman present, which was resented by Mr. Gilbert on the spot. Pistols were drawn on both sides and nine shots exchanged, five of which took effect, injuring Mr. Gilbert and his brother, as well as two of Messrs. Clement, but none of them seriously.*[173]

According to Clement, however, the attack was unprovoked. He said "that while sitting quietly engaged in a conversation with a gentleman he was fired upon by Wm. Gilbert a person implicated in his domestic difficulties and severely wounded while in a sitting posture."[174] Not surprisingly, this confrontation did nothing to quell the ill feeling between either Victoria and James or their families and friends. And despite the gravity of this near fatal meeting, it was only to be a rehearsal for what was to come.

By February 1860, the tensions between the Clement and Smith families had heightened to the extreme. During the separation, James had taken their young daughter to live with his relatives. Learning of this, Victoria's grandfather Captain Vincent Witcher became incensed and had the daughter removed and reunited with Victoria.[175]

A successful businessman, lawyer and former president of the Richmond and Danville Railroad, Captain Witcher, who was seventy-eight at the time, had been a good friend of James's father—Dr. George Clement, a physician and prominent farmer. But their warm relationship did nothing to cool Witcher's anger toward his friend's son. He fully supported his granddaughter's petition for divorce and planned to attend the next deposition meeting.[176]

Before further depositions were to be taken, James decided to draw up a will. He was convinced that he would be assassinated either by Gilbert or one of Victoria's brothers and wanted his wishes made clear upon his death:

> *I James R. Clement of the County of Franklin and State of Virginia contemplating the end of life from assassination or attack from my enemies such as I experienced at Sandy Level in the county of Pittsylvania on the 14th Inst but being of sound and disposing mind and memory do make this my last will and testament hereby revoking all others.*[177]

Victoria was to receive nothing from his estate, except that which was required to care for their child.[178]

On a spring day, the two families and friends met to give their depositions regarding the marriage between James and Victoria Clement. But given what had transpired at the first meeting, everyone who attended came armed with pistols and Bowie knives. Captain Witcher was armed with a revolver. Accompanying him was his son Addison Witcher, his grandsons John A. Smith and Vincent Oliver Smith—brothers of Victoria—and his son-in-law Samuel Swanson. James had brought along his two brothers—William and Ralph. The meeting took place in the back room of Dickinson's Store near the Pittsylvania County line.[179]

As the depositions were being taken, Witcher reportedly asked a question or made a caustic remark that offended Ralph Clement. In the course of a few seconds, pistols were pulled and shots fired. A ball passed through Captain Witcher's wrist and into his elbow, but he was not seriously injured.[180]

The Clement brothers were not so lucky. Witcher had managed to fire several shots, immediately killing James and fatally wounding his brothers William and Ralph. John A. Smith received a ball to the shoulder during the fray, but apparently, he was able to stab William Clement five times to the neck, chest and abdomen. It was later determined that it was these stab wounds rather than Witcher's pistol that had probably killed him.[181]

Soon after the confrontation, the Witchers and the Smiths surrendered themselves into the custody of the Franklin County sheriff. But fearful that friends and family members of the Clements would seek revenge, Vincent Witcher refused to disarm. The possible danger to Witcher was real, and given the fact that he was a well-respected and influential gentleman in Franklin County, he was allowed to remain armed throughout the forthcoming preliminary hearing.[182]

At the hearing in March 1860, five judges were assembled to hear the evidence against the Witchers, Smiths and Swanson. The killing had aroused much interest in the county. Both the Witcher and Clement families were prominent citizens and were well known not only to the people of Franklin but also to those who lived in the surrounding counties.

Before a large crowd in the courthouse in Rocky Mount, lawyers for the defense and the commonwealth's attorney debated the facts of the case. After much deliberation, three of the five judges concluded that there was no evidence of who fired the first shot. And since there was also no proof of premeditation on the part of the defendants, Vincent Oliver Witcher, John Smith, Vincent Oliver Smith and Samuel Swanson were acquitted of all charges.[183]

~ ~ ~ ~ ~ ~ ~

The Clement-Witcher killings were one of the most sensational feuds in Franklin County's history. Although less famous, there were many more that were just as bloody. Newspapers and court records during the late nineteenth and early twentieth centuries often contained reports of families in Franklin and neighboring counties settling their differences with rival families not with litigation or mediation but with gunplay. Such confrontations invariably led to shootouts that left two or three men dead.

In January 1905, members of the Abshire and Laprad families decided to meet on common ground at the home of Drury Hanes near Callaway and settle their long-standing differences. But during the exchange, someone insulted the wife of one of the men. What followed would make the "Shootout at the O.K. Coral" look like little more than a neighborhood squabble, albeit a violent one:

> *After the first round had been fired and the smoke cleared away, it was found that the two Abshires and Laprad were lying on the ground wounded. One of the Abshires managed to raise himself up on his elbows and, after reloading his breech-loading shotgun, turned upon his wounded antagonist, Laprad, who lay nearby, and pointing the weapon at him, fired. The load took effect in his neck, completely severing the head from the body.*[184]

Since no one could determine who fired first, no one was arrested or charged for the killing.

In another confrontation three years later, in May 1908, two families— the Sheltons and the Massies—came to blows just over the Franklin County line in a little valley near Philpott in Henry County. There apparently had been bad blood between the two families for a long time. The Sheltons believed the Massie clan had cut up several of their stills and were determined to retaliate.[185]

Armed with shotguns, pistols and axes, the Sheltons approached the home of Herford Spencer, where the Massies, they had learned, were staying. As the Sheltons approached the Spencer home, the wife of Herford Spencer "waved a bonnet or a handkerchief...this being the signal that precipitated the shooting." The battle that ensued left Samuel Shelton, James Holly and Charles Dodson dead. William and Grover Massie were arrested and charged with murder, but they pleaded self-defense and were later acquitted of the crime.[186]

In February 1927, just over the line in Patrick County, rival moonshine factions and families battled to the death over who would hold sway over illegal distilling in the mountains. Certain that Turner Hall had reported their still to the authorities, Maynard and David Cox destroyed Hall's still in retaliation. It was then that the two factions met not far from the Cox home. Although federal authorities said that no one had squealed on their fellow moonshiners, the Cox brothers were not convinced.[187]

Meeting in Dodson, just two or three miles from the Franklin County line, the two factions opened fire on one another. Maynard and David Cox, along with Turner Hall, died in the shootout. Given that the Dodson vicinity was alleged to be one of the most prolific in terms of moonshining, few people were willing to provide any information regarding the gun battle. No one was arrested or convicted for the killings.[188]

Were the men of Franklin County and neighboring counties more prone to violence than those in other parts of Virginia or the nation? Perhaps not. But it is true that the people who lived in the mountainous sections of Franklin County and other areas of the Blue Ridge were predominantly of Scots-Irish ancestry.

Often described as clannish and quick to anger, there is much antidotal evidence that they were inclined to violence, particularly if they felt they or their families had been insulted or wronged in some way. To say this, however, is to risk, justifiably, stereotyping a people. But scholars who have studied Celtic cultures seem to agree that the Scots-Irish were "born fighting."[189]

~ ~ ~ ~ ~ ~ ~

It was not unusual for men in Franklin County to resort to violence when they felt their property rights had not been respected. On one June day in 1870, for example, an argument erupted between two men over a dog. According to the *Richmond Dispatch*, Cyrus Lavender's dog killed a sheep belonging to a young man named Joplin. In retaliation, Joplin killed Lavender's dog. This led to a violent confrontation at the Franklin County Courthouse between Joplin and Lavender's allies.[190]

Robert C. Henderson, a local magistrate, tried to stop the fight before someone got killed. Unfortunately, Henderson was drawn into the violence when George Lavender, Cyrus's father, attempted to strike him with his crutch "and seizing the crutch, he repelled the attack of its owner, and in the confusion and excitement of the moment struck him a lick with his own crutch which felled him and resulted in his death." Henderson and two other men, Otho Joplin and John J. Saunders, were indicted for Lavender's killing, but they all were acquitted of the charge.[191]

Disputes between neighbors over boundaries between their farms could also turn bloody. In February 1882, Wiley Tench and his neighbor, a man identified as a Mr. Parker, got into a dispute over the placement of a fence between their properties. As the discussion became heated, Tench drew a pistol. But Parker's son, who was present, recognized the danger and struck Tench over the head with a rock. The blow, however, did little to deter Tench. He managed to fire several shots, one of which killed the elder Parker.[192]

Men like Tench and Parker were quick to draw weapons to prevent anyone from encroaching or trespassing on their land. Such was the case with John Keller and James Hopkins. On September 28, 1902, the two Franklin County farmers got into argument over Hopkins trespassing on Keller's land. As the exchange grew more heated, Kessler drew his pistol and shot Hopkins, leaving him seriously wounded.[193]

Henry C. Motley, who owned a large plantation near the Pittsylvania line, became enraged one July day in 1907 when he saw Henry Adams and his young Black farmhand George Dutton drive their wagon across his land. Motley grabbed a shotgun to confront Adams, who was armed with a pistol. With Motley was his young daughter and wife.[194]

Adams and Motley almost immediately came to blows. During the course of the scuffle, the two men seized each other's weapons. Adams, according to Dutton's testimony, yelled for him to grab his pistol from Motley. Once freed from Motley, Dutton took the pistol and fled. As he ran from the scene, a rock, said Dutton, "whizzed by him and he turned and shot three- or four-times killing Motley." Both Dutton and Adams were arrested and charged.[195]

~ ~ ~ ~ ~ ~ ~

There seemed to be an epidemic of killing and gun violence even within Franklin County families between 1901 and 1904. On December 6, 1901, James Morrison decided to resolve a dispute with his brother-in-law James McCoy at the sawmill where McCoy worked. Both drunk and angry at McCoy, Morrison threatened to kill the other employees and shoot McCoy. In response, McCoy grabbed an iron square and struck McCoy over the head, crushing his skull. He died soon after.[196]

Later that December on a Sunday morning at Coles Creek, about six miles west of Rocky Mount, an altercation occurred between David Cannady and his father-in-law, Martin Akers, that resulted in Akers's death. During breakfast, Akers, who boarded with his daughter and son-in-law, became so quarrelsome and irascible that Cannaday left the table. According to Cannaday, as he started out the door, he told Akers that he would have to find another place to live if he did not behave himself.[197]

Akers became enraged and threw a chair at Cannady. The chair missed Cannaday, but feeling threatened, "he gathered a large rock used to stop the cathole under the door, and struck the old man on the head, fracturing his skull." After Akers died later that afternoon, Cannaday turned himself into the authorities and pleaded self-defense.[198]

In January 1902, Lewis Bridges's brother and brother-in-law attacked him "without provocation." One of his assailants hit him with a rock. According to the *Roanoke Times*, he "was cut as was his daughter who was with him." Guns were drawn and Lewis Bridges killed both his brother and his brother-in-law. The reason given for the attack, said Bridges, was that his brother and brother-in-law were angry that he found them offensive and would have little or nothing to do with them.[199]

Three years later, bad blood between two family members led to a tragic killing. Chap Ramsey and his nephew Williard had long-standing differences, and on one fall day, those differences finally led to gunplay. During the course of an argument, Chap, who felt threated, drew his gun and fired on Willard, killing him instantly. Fearing that members of his own family would lynch him for killing Willard, Chap fled the area. He later turned himself in to the Franklin County sheriff.[200]

~ ~ ~ ~ ~ ~ ~

Wherever people gathered in Franklin County—church picnics, dances, weddings and other community events—there was always the possibility of violence between men, especially when whiskey was involved. At a "basket picnic" on an August day in 1902, for example, R. Snyder, who had been drinking, got into an argument with a man named Dalton. Dalton's son, who also was at the picnic, felt that his father was being bullied and insulted.[201]

The younger Dalton finally had had enough and knocked Snyder to the ground with a blow to the face. Before Snyder was able to regain his feet, Dalton "dealt him two severe blows to the head with a wagon brake stick." For the next few days, Snyder lay close to death. Whether he survived is uncertain.[202]

Passions could become particularly inflamed at a political meeting, resulting in brawling or, worse yet, homicide. During a political debate in

Rocky Mount in 1880, a "bloody row" occurred between those who favored the Readjusters and those who supported the Conservative Democratic Party. The Readjusters, led by former Confederate general William Mahone, advocated readjusting or only paying a portion of the principal and interest of the prewar state debt. They argued that this would free up money for schools, roads and other projects. Conservative Democrats saw this as a dangerously radical proposal that would hurt the state's standing with creditors.

> *Yesterday was a big day at Rocky Mount, Franklin County....Later in the day J. Tony Stovall insulted Hon. George C. Cabell from the stand. Mr. Cabell demanded an apology, and then Stovall's friends gave the signal and rushed for the stand. Mr. Cabell was stricken down by a cowardly blow from the rear. This fired the crowd, and in less than one minute Stovall and his Radical henchmen were carried off the ground bruised and bleeding. A general row ensued, and many bloody faces graced the court green, but there was no serious injury. Stovall's head is much damaged and Lee Wilson, a Radical, is in no better condition.*[203]

Such confrontations were not uncommon during the nineteenth century, especially in the South. There was much conflict over the future of the region and how to recover from the devastation of the Civil War. The stakes were high, and for many, including those in Franklin County, politics was a blood sport.

There was always potential for trouble at community events, particularly when a young man felt another was attempting to steal his love interest. At a corn shucking and dance at the home of Jim Whitaker on Chestnut Knob Mountain, a gun and knife fight broke out between Sam Hairston and Tom Dodson. Hairston "objected to Dodson waltzing with his sweetheart, and went at him with an open knife." Friends of the two men became involved, and soon what was to be a joyous evening turned into a bloody mêlée:

> *Dodson drew a revolver and fired at this rival. Penn, who is a friend of Hairston's, rushed up with a pistol and shot Dodson several times. Dodson fell to the floor, where upon his cousin, Ben Reamy, went to his assistance, and grabbing his pistol, fired on Penn, wounding him in the side. Hairston then turned upon Reamy with his knife and inflicted half a dozen deep gashes across his face and chest. Dodson was cut across the abdomen with a knife in the hands of Hairston, and was shot four times by Penn, twice*

in the side, once in the neck, and once in the groin. He cannot live. Reamy may recover, but his chances are slim. Penn's wounds are slight. Hairston was shot in the leg, and Ed Franch, a bystander, was hit in the cheek by a stray bullet. Hairston and Penn have been arrested.[204]

That more people were not hit and seriously injured is remarkable. Needless to say, the dance came to an abrupt halt.

~ ~ ~ ~ ~ ~ ~

SHERIFFS AND COMMONWEALTH ATTORNEYS worked hard to bring troublemakers and murderers to justice but were met with resistance at every turn. People in the mountainous sections of the county were unwilling to cooperate with the authorities, especially those they saw as outsiders.

C. Carter Lee, a grandnephew of Robert E. Lee, for example, came to the county in 1928 at the age of twenty-three and assumed the office of commonwealth's attorney. Yet despite his Virginia pedigree, Lee discovered that the people of Franklin County were very closemouthed about the goings-on in their communities and had their own beliefs regarding right and wrong.

Mountain men, he soon learned, had very pronounced notions of personal honor and were quick to turn to violence if they felt they had been in any way slighted or insulted. In a 1930 article, the *Times Dispatch* in Richmond recounted the obstacles that Lee and other law enforcement officers faced in trying to bring law and order to the county:

> *Even Mr. Lee can do no more than estimate the number of murders which have been committed in this county since he assumed the Office of Commonwealth's attorney in 1928. The farmers and mountain folk of Franklin County are hot-tempered, impetuous people, still no more impregnated by the patient but certain processes of "civilized" law. They have their own code of justice, in which death plays a frequent and important part. When roused to anger, they reach swiftly and blindly for their guns.*[205]

Despite his best efforts and "resolute temperament," Lee, said the article, had been able to secure only a few convictions for murder during his tenure in office.[206]

In all of the cases that Lee brought to trial, he "had to fight the secretiveness of those people, their reluctance to give evidence against men who have followed their own code in killing, and he has had to fight for the sympathy of his jurors toward men concerning whose guilt there could be no reasonable doubt."[207] Ironically, Lee, as earlier noted, was charged in the Great Moonshine Conspiracy Trial with taking advantage of the mountain code of silence in a scheme to allow moonshiners to operate as long as they paid for the privilege.

Chapter 8

HONOR AND THE UNWRITTEN LAW

It was a hot August day in 1907 in Ferrum when Lucy Wimmer laid to rest her daughter Pepsie and her son-in-law L.J. Wingfield in the family cemetery. Not far from their grave site was that of her husband, Mark, who had been murdered in an ambush near the town some sixteen years earlier. No one was arrested or convicted of the crime. Sadly, like her father, Pepsie too had been murdered, not by an unknown assailant but by her own husband.[208]

Pepsie had always been something of a wild child and had run away to Roanoke when she was just sixteen. It was there that she met L.J., who was a conductor with the Norfolk and Western Railway. When he transferred to Maryland, she followed and, soon after, married him in Cumberland. Young and naïve, she thought that a railroad man would be quite a catch. L.J. had a good job with a steady income that would afford her an opportunity to escape the poverty and isolation of her mountain home in Franklin County.[209]

It was not long, however, before Pepsie and L.J. began to quarrel. He was extremely jealous and was suspicious of any man who paid the slightest attention to her. His suspicions grew worse after they returned to Roanoke in early July 1907. Hoping to escape what was becoming an unbearable situation, she reached out to W.C. Turner, an old family friend who also worked for Norfolk and Western.[210]

Her appeal for help, however, only fueled L.J.'s jealousy. He believed that Turner and Pepsie were lovers and that she planned to run away with him. Despite Turner's insistence that he was a friend who was merely responding to a request for advice, L.J. was not to be dissuaded. Turner had invaded his home and alienated his wife's affections. He made it known that he would kill Turner on sight.[211]

Convinced that the threat was real, Turner had L.J. arrested. But it was not long before L.J. made bail and returned home. Turner feared the worse. L.J. was unhinged and might kill not only him but also Pepsie.[212]

His fears were realized on the afternoon of August 8. As Pepsie washed clothes on the back porch of their home on Park Street in Roanoke, L.J. flew into a rage and struck her repeatedly. L.J. dragged her into the house as she screamed, "Do not kill me!" It was soon afterward that neighbors heard five shots, the first three in succession.[213]

When the police arrived, they found Pepsie lying on the bed with two gunshots to her head. L.J. was lying next to her on the floor. He had cut his throat. A pool of blood in the living room indicated that after L.J. killed Pepsie, he moved her body to the adjoining room and placed it on the bed. It was then, as he stood over his murdered wife, that he killed himself.[214]

L.J. left a note stating that both Turner and "bad women were the cause of me doing this." He also claimed that he "had sacrificed all for her" and that he wanted the couple "buried in the same coffin with my head on her breast." This seemed to be at odds with a receipt from a law firm the police found in his papers. L.J. had apparently begun divorce proceedings against Pepsie.[215]

Pepsie's mother, not surprisingly, did not honor L.J.'s request. In fact, she tried to find relatives or friends of her son-in-law who might claim the body. No one, however, came forward. She decided, albeit reluctantly, to bury him beside her daughter in the Wimmer family cemetery in Ferrum.[216]

~ ~ ~ ~ ~ ~ ~

ON NOVEMBER 1, 1908, Dr. James Semple Cahill, a twenty-seven-year-old dentist, loaded two pistols and walked to the Norfolk and Western train station in Rocky Mount. Searching the large crowd that was waiting to board the train, he spotted George "Bob" Robert Smithers, a forty-year-old traveling salesman who lived nearby. Yelling "I am in the right!" Cahill fired both of his pistols at Smithers. Also armed, Smithers returned the fire, hitting Cahill but once in the leg. Cahill's shots, however, had found their mark. Smithers lay bleeding from five bullet wounds, including one to the groin. He would die two days later.[217]

Cahill had made it known for several months that he would kill Smithers on sight. His wife, Marie, had left him, and Smithers, he believed, was

The Rocky Mount passenger depot where Dr. James Cahill shot Bob Smithers was a central place for local residents to travel to cities throughout the region. *Courtesy of the Town of Rocky Mount.*

responsible. For several months, she had been making visits to Smithers's sister Anna, a seamstress who lived with Bob in Rocky Mount. Marie explained that she frequently had to meet with Anna in order to get proper fittings for her clothes. A neighbor, however, witnessed Marie's comings and goings when Bob was at home and told Cahill that he suspected her of having an inappropriate relationship with Smithers.[218]

Cahill was immediately arrested and charged with murder. As he was well respected in the community, many offered to assist him with bail. But given the severity of the charge, Judge Campbell refused to grant bail—even the $100,000 put up by many prominent citizens. Cahill, however, did secure three established Southwest Virginia attorneys to represent him: Congressman E.W. Saunders, Colonel Peter Hairston Dillard and Carter Lee Dillard.[219]

Cahill's attorneys did not dispute the facts of the case—clearly, he went to the train station to kill Smithers. But Cahill, they argued, believed he had been cuckolded and was suffering from temporary insanity at the time. This defense, together with the "unwritten law"—the right of a husband to take revenge on a man who had alienated his wife's affections—would be their best argument for an acquittal.[220]

There was every reason to believe that this strategy might be successful. Psychiatrists—or alienists, as they were then called—were prepared to testify that Dr. Cahill was "mentally unbalanced." Even neighbors from his former home in Henry County would testify that his family had a history of insanity. But perhaps more important, Virginia juries had never convicted a man for killing the seducer of his wife.[221]

In 1900, for example, Captain Mike Prince of the Norfolk police saw his longtime friend and political ally Charles Cannon on the street between the Citizens Bank and the federal customhouse. Walking up to him, Prince told Charley that he wanted to speak with him. Prince then put his hand on Charles's arm, and the two walked to the yard of the customhouse. Nothing seemed to be amiss as they talked quietly. But then Prince pushed Charles away and drew his .32-caliber pistol. After firing once into his friend's chest and then again at his head, Prince turned to walk away.[222]

By then, Cannon was lying facedown in the customhouse yard. Hearing gunshots, citizens rushed to the scene, but it was too late for Cannon. Prince walked over to his prostrate body and put a bullet into the back of his head.[223]

The citizens of Norfolk were shocked. What could have possessed Prince to murder his best friend? What was revealed during Prince's trial convinced them that he was justified in killing Charles Cannon.[224]

From a series of anonymous letters, Prince had learned that Cannon and his wife had been having sexual relations for over two years. Cannon's wife, he later learned, was the author of the letters. Incensed, Prince compelled his wife to confess to her infidelity. However, the story she told was not one of romance but one of seduction on the part of Cannon. According to Mrs. Prince, Cannon had taken advantage of her. Fearing that Cannon would tell her husband, she continued the relationship, thinking that one day she would be able to extricate herself from his clutches.[225]

Prince's wife's confession convinced him that Charles had sullied his marriage bed and that he must make restitution. But what enraged him even more was that Cannon had said that he was not the only one to have enjoyed his wife's affections. According to Cannon, Mrs. Prince was a regular at his bar and was quite popular with the young blades who frequented his establishment.[226]

Prince faced the very real possibility of execution if convicted. But his lawyer, R.T. Thorpe, believed that a defense that included both the "unwritten law" and temporary insanity would win his client an acquittal. To support this defense, Thorpe maintained that no jury in Virginia or the United States had ever convicted a man for murder when that man killed another man for defiling his wife, mother or daughter.[227]

The most famous case he cited was that of New York congressman Dan Sickles, who in 1859 killed his wife's lover Philip Barton Key, the son of Francis Scott Key, in Lafayette Square just across the street from the White House in Washington, D.C. Sickles was immediately arrested and charged with murder. But because of his standing in the Democratic Party and his considerable wealth, he was able to assemble a veritable who's who of legal experts and politicians to defend him, one of whom was Edwin Stanton, the future secretary of war.[228]

It was this team, led by Stanton, that argued that Sickles was not guilty by reason of temporary insanity. This defense, never before used in the United States, maintained that Sickles was so distraught over his wife's infidelity that he lost all control of his faculties and killed the man who had brought dishonor to his home.[229]

Accepting this argument, the presiding judge instructed the jury members to consider Sickles's state of mind at the time he killed Key. After only an hour of deliberation, they returned a verdict of not guilty. It was a victory not only for the temporary insanity defense but also for the prevailing notion that a husband had a right, maybe even a duty, to defend his family and society against men such as Key.[230]

Using the precedent of the Sickles decision, Thorpe stated in his closing argument that the killing was justified, particularly since Virginia law did little or nothing to protect a husband from a man who had transgressed his home and family:

> *The District Attorney tells you that the law provides punishment for the adulterer. He tells you that a scoundrel may invade your home, debauch your wife and escape with a paltry fine of $20.00. But when the outraged husband has taken the law into his own hands and meted out to the scoundrel his richly deserved punish-ment, there was never gibbet in Virginia or America on which a man like that was executed.*[231]

Prince, he said, "did what was right." He confronted the "slimy reprobate" and told him what his wife had confessed. But Cannon not only "admitted his guilt, but with a maddening sneer said: 'I'm not the only one.'" This, said Thorpe, sent Prince over the edge:

89

What could Prince do? Gentleman, under the technical law, you cannot hang this man, for the evidence demonstrates that he was mentally irresponsible. And gentleman, if you hang him, you rob the gibbet of its ignominy and make of it a martyr's cross where men are crucified for doing that which they ought to do.[232]

In his final remarks, Thorpe asked the members of the jury to put themselves in Prince's place. Given the shame and disgrace that Cannon brought to his family, he had only two choices: "Kill himself or kill the vile author of his ruin."[233]

The jury members retired to their chambers and deliberated. After an hour and ten minutes, the jury returned a verdict. "We the jury find the prisoner, Michael H. Prince," read the foreman, "not guilty as charged in the indictment." The courtroom erupted in applause and men rushed to shake Prince's hand. All agreed it appeared that Cannon had violated the sanctity of Prince's home and, in so doing, had brought about his own demise.[234]

Virginia newspapers lauded the jury's decision. The written law, said editors, provided insufficient punishment for men such as Cannon. The only just punishment for Cannon and his ilk, said the *Virginian-Pilot*, a Norfolk paper, was a swift and certain death.

Society does not exist by the written law alone. The unwritten law in Virginia is that the husband is justifiable in taking the life of the man who debauches his wife, wrecks his home, stains his honor and makes their mother's name a shame to his children. The unwritten law says the punishment should be death; the written law says it is a $20 fine. The husband who would take his case into court, under such circumstances, would be lashed with the scorn and contempt of his fellows to the end of his wretched existence.[235]

The paper called on the General Assembly to make a husband or a father's killing of a man who "desecrated his hearthstone" a justifiable homicide in the same way it already did for a man acting in self-defense.[236]

Seven years after the Prince case, William Loving, a former judge of Nelson County, killed Theodore Estes, the son of the local sheriff, at his job at a fertilizer company in 1907. Convinced that he had plied his daughter with a drug-laced dram of alcohol and then taken advantage of her, Loving killed the unsuspecting Estes with two blasts from his shotgun.[237]

Arrested on the charge of murder in the first degree, Loving had but one defense—the unwritten law. Estes, said his attorneys, had assaulted the judge's daughter, and he, as a Virginia gentleman and a man of honor, had no other recourse but to right the wrong that was done to his family. The jury deliberated for only forty-five minutes and returned a verdict of not guilty.[238]

It was the precedent set in the Loving and Prince cases that would win the day for Cahill. After several postponements, the trial finally got underway in April 1910, and as expected, Cahill entered a plea of not guilty by reason of insanity. The jury members listened to witnesses and the testimony of mental health experts. They also visited the train station where the killing occurred. When they reconvened, they deliberated for only ten minutes and returned a verdict of not guilty.[239]

Linda Stanley, a Franklin County historian and former reporter, details much of the story of Dr. Cahill in volume three of her series *Franklin County Killin'*. According to Stanley, there is no record of Dr. Cahill ever receiving treatment for mental illness. In fact, soon after his acquittal he returned to his dental practice in Rocky Mount. He later left his practice, joined the U.S. Army Dental Corps and served in the reserves during World War I. How long he served is uncertain. What is known, says Stanley, is that at the time of his enlistment, he was living in the Richmond home of Walter Lee Hopkins, a Franklin County native whom he must have known from his years in Rocky Mount.[240]

Cahill died in 1948 at the age of sixty-eight from a cerebral hemorrhage. Hopkins served as the executor of his estate, which was valued at $51,000. According to his will, his daughter, Virginia Cahill Himmelwright, who apparently was his only child, was to receive $25 per month from the estate. He is buried in Arlington National Cemetery.[241]

Chapter 9

GETTING AWAY WITH MURDER

In November 1901, William Hale, a Black man, became enraged by remarks made by some of the speakers at a Democratic political rally in Ferrum. The Democratic Party controlled the state, and the speakers proposed amending the Virginia constitution to require a poll tax and a literacy test to vote. Designed to limit Black participation in elections, Black citizens of the state condemned the measures.

Visibly angry, Hale began quarreling with some of the attendees. He soon left the area and returned with a double-barreled shotgun loaded with buckshot and fired into the crowd. He killed J.A. Robinette, the local blacksmith and John Thomas, another Ferrum resident. Two other men were seriously wounded.[242]

Hale fled to the mountains about six miles from Ferrum with his brother-in-law Larkin Saunders. Armed with shotguns and Winchester rifles, the two battled a posse of county men. Saunders was wounded during the exchange and was captured. Hale, however, managed to escape.[243]

White folks in Ferrum were so outraged that many of its Black citizens feared that they might be targeted for retaliation. The danger was real. A Black man who injured or killed a white man, even in self-defense, was a threat to Jim Crow segregation in the South. It was believed by many that such an act of defiance must be swiftly and mercilessly punished lest others forget their place and rise up against the white community.

But in some communities, this was not enough, and innocent Black people could be terrorized and driven from their homes. Thankfully this did not happen in Ferrum. Nevertheless, reported the *Richmond Times Dispatch*, "the people of Forrum [*sic*] are and have been very much incensed and had the negro been captured at the time he would have probably been lynched."[244]

Many in the county thought they would have an opportunity to exact their revenge when news reached them in April 1902 that a man fitting Hale's description had been arrested in Louisiana and was awaiting extradition. Much to their chagrin, he turned out to be the wrong man. Despite reported sightings of Hale and rumors as to his whereabouts, there are no court records or newspaper reports of his ever being captured or lynched.[245]

~ ~ ~ ~ ~ ~ ~

IN JULY 1905, MAURICE Francis hitched his horse to his buggy outside his home in Roanoke and began the forty-mile trek to Gracie Link's home in Simpsons just over the county line in Floyd. Maurice had been courting Gracie for some time, and finally, she had agreed to marry him. But within a mile from her house, he was suddenly hit with a full load of buckshot. His horse was also hit but managed to break free from the buggy. When the bleeding horse was later spotted with the shafts from the buggy still attached to him, concerned neighbors searched the area for Maurice. Although he was still alive when discovered in the buggy, he had only a short time left to live.[246]

He was removed to a nearby home where a Dr. Thomas tried to treat his wounds. But the blast had peppered his body with shot and the bleeding could not be stopped. Before he succumbed to his wounds, Francis told Thomas that he did not see who shot him, but he believed it was John Richards, who had been his rival for Gracie's affections. John Connor, who found Francis after the shooting, also said that he told him that he believed Richards was his killer. Gracie confirmed this. Francis's dying words, she told authorities were "that jealousy was an awful thing, Richards."[247]

John Richards was twenty-two, lived in Floyd County and taught school there while he took classes at the University of Virginia. The son of James Richards, a schoolteacher and prosperous farmer in Simpsons, located not far from Callaway, he hoped to leave teaching and complete a medical degree at the University of Virginia. He had also hoped that Gracie would one day become his wife.[248]

The evidence against John Richards included not only Francis's dying statement but also his well-known jealousy of his rival for Gracie's affections and the fact that he was spotted near the murder scene sitting on a fence with a double-barreled shotgun in his lap. There were witnesses who also claimed that he was seen in the vicinity of the killing wearing a false mustache and an overcoat. It was a poor attempt at a disguise, said one witness. He knew Richards well and was not fooled.[249]

Citizens in the community of Simpsons, where the murder occurred, were incensed and believed Richards was the killer. A well-armed crowd assembled and threatened to hang him if found. With the help of his father and brother, Richards hid from the mob and then fled to Ferrum. Once he was informed that he would not be harmed, he returned home to await arrest.[250]

The constable sent to arrest Richards at his Floyd County home the day following the murder testified that he found Richards and his father hiding in a thicket near their house. While the two escaped to a swamp, he was able to follow their tracks for some distance. He was unable to apprehend the two, but he did discover that the tracks made by one of the men were the same size as those leading from the site where Francis was killed.[251]

The commonwealth's attorney believed the preponderance of evidence, although circumstantial, would result in a speedy conviction. To his dismay, this was not to be the case. While he and most of the citizens of Floyd and Franklin County were convinced of his guilt, the jury in two separate trials remained deadlocked.[252]

In a third trial held in Patrick County, the jury returned a verdict of guilty of murder in the first degree, and he was sentenced to be hanged. But the verdict had little impact on the young teacher. As the judge read the verdict and his death sentence, Richards laughed. He and his attorneys would appeal to the Virginia Supreme Court and be granted a new trial.[253]

Although Richards's father, mother, sister and brother had testified in the first two trials that he was at home when the murder occurred, they were now dead, tragically, from complications stemming from pneumonia. His defense now rested on the testimony of friends and relatives who said he was not at the spot where Francis was killed on that July day in 1905. Without an eyewitness, the prosecution could not prove that he was actually in the vicinity of the murder. As a result, the fourth trial ended in a hung jury.[254]

In the fifth and final trial in August 1908, the jury, after deliberating only twenty minutes, returned a verdict of not guilty. Angered by the verdict, Maurice's brother tried to shoot Richards in the courtroom. One of the prosecuting attorneys, however, intervened and disarmed him. Richards quickly left the courthouse in a waiting buggy.[255]

But who killed Francis? It clearly was not a case of robbery, and there were no signs of a struggle at the scene. Was it an accident? There was no evidence to suggest that Francis was the unfortunate victim of a hunting mishap. On the contrary, his wounds indicated that he was shot at close range, so it was highly unlikely that his killing was accidental. Francis was, no doubt, targeted for assassination.

Despite his acquittal, most believed that Richards was the likely killer. He had motive, and he was seen in the vicinity of Francis's death. Nevertheless, Francis's murder would go unsolved. But in the minds of Gracie and the people of Floyd and Franklin County, Richards had gotten away with murder.

~ ~ ~ ~ ~ ~ ~

It was a warm July day in 1907 when Ed Saul, while out hunting, walked past Hattie Ramsey's home near Henry. Ed was smitten with Hattie and hoped that she might agree to marry him some day. But Hattie had other suitors, one of whom was his friend Marshall King.

From the path close to the house, Saul could see that Hattie was entertaining someone in her parlor. As he moved closer for a better view, he saw that it was Marshall. Concealing his weapon, he then went to the front door and asked King to step outside. Since the two young men had been childhood friends, King believed he had no reason to fear Ed. Unfortunately, he was mistaken.[256]

Saul told King that he needed to speak with him and asked that he walk with him to the woods behind the barn. Hattie's mother was a bit suspicious and asked her son-in-law, Calvin Scarborough, to follow them. As he neared the two men, he could see that Ed was pointing a shotgun at Marshall's back. "Don't do that Ed, wait!" he screamed. Realizing now that he was about to be shot, Marshall pleaded for his life. But Ed's mind was made up, and he pulled the trigger. The blast hit Marshall square in the back, instantly killing him. In a voice loud enough for Hattie and her family to hear from the house, Ed yelled, "Goodbye, folks, I'm gone!"[257]

Once notified of the killing, Sheriff David Nicholson and his deputies immediately began a search for Saul. People who knew Saul said that they had seen him heading in the direction of Martinsville the day of the murder. But a search of the city and Henry County turned up nothing. Perhaps he had fled to North Carolina or was hiding in West Virginia, where he had previously worked. It was also possible that he had taken a train to a city outside the region.[258]

As days and weeks passed with no sign of Ed, Marshall's family and friends became increasingly frustrated and offered a seventy-five-dollar reward for his capture. Sheriff Nicholson himself put up twenty-five dollars.[259]

Yet despite the considerable sum offered at the time, no one came forward with credible information as to Ed's whereabouts. For years following the murder, there were reported sightings of men who fit Ed's description. But they, like other promising clues, led nowhere. Ed had vanished.

Or had he? In 1930, Lola Philpott Walker, a Franklin County woman who lived in Ashland, Kentucky, identified a man held in an Ashland jail as Ed Saul. The man, who said his name was Ira "Jack" Turner, worked as a jockey and often gave Lola and her husband tips on horses. Although she eventually recognized the man as Saul, she decided that it was not her place to report him to the authorities.[260]

Turner, said Lola, feared that she might reveal his true identity to the authorities. This, she believed, was why he turned up outside her house one evening—drunk and visibly confused. The police arrested Turner and charged him with public drunkenness and disorderly behavior. But the man seemed to think that he was actually being held for some other crime and made frequent references to a killing. But what killing? Finally, she decided to tell them that he was Ed Saul and was wanted by the Franklin County Sheriff's Department for the murder of Marshall King in 1907.[261]

How could she be sure that this man was actually Saul? "I know he is Saul," she asserted in a newspaper interview. "I knew him when he was 15 years old. He used to play cards with my brother. He can't be anybody named Ira Turner." Lola further explained that she attended school with both Ed and Marshall in Henry and knew them intimately.[262]

When Sheriff John Peter Hodges got notice that the man in the Ashland jail had been identified as Ed Saul, he got papers to extradite him to Franklin County. The man, however, insisted that he was Ira J. Turner from Rockingham County, Virginia, and knew nothing of Saul or the murder of Marshall King. The sheriff and Commonwealth's Attorney C. Carter Lee thought that it was possible that the man was telling the truth. Nevertheless, they placed him in a cell in Rocky Mount until they could verify his identity.[263]

But that was to prove difficult. Once notified, friends and family members from Rockingham County, including his father, came to Rocky Mount to identify the man in the cell. Although they had not seen him in years, they all stated unequivocally that he was Ira Turner. Yet half of the residents of Henry who had a chance to see the man maintained that he was undoubtedly Ed Saul. Sheriff Hodges and Carter Lee were perplexed. Lee, however, decided to prosecute the man he believed to be Ed Saul for the murder of Marshall King.[264]

But just as he began preparing his case, a number of key witnesses stated that the man in the cell was definitely not Ed Saul. Elsie Gore, Hattie Ramsey's sister, for example, traveled all the way from Arizona just to tell Sheriff Hodges and Carter Lee that they had the wrong man. Hattie herself visited the man in his cell and concluded that he was not Saul. Saul's brother and sister even testified that the man was not Ed.[265]

And then there was E.C. Payne, a retired Washington detective who had lived with Saul and his two brothers in a boardinghouse kept by the Ramsey sisters in 1907. After learning that a man was being held in Franklin County as Ed Saul, he decided to tell the *Richmond Times Dispatch* what he knew of Saul and the murder of Marshall King. According to Payne, the man in the Rocky Mount jail was definitely not Saul. "I'd know Ed Saul's skin if it were in a boot and recognize his hide in a tanyard, and that man in the Franklin County jail is not Ed Saul," he exclaimed. Payne maintained that he had seen Saul on a number of occasions since the murder, including once at a Raleigh, North Carolina drugstore. He was certain that he was still alive, but this man was not him.[266]

Payne presented the *Richmond Times Dispatch* with a written description he had of Saul when he was arrested in connection with a murder in 1906: "Ed Saul. Age 22. Weight 162. Eyes and hair brown. Sallow complexion. Five feet nine and one-half inches tall. Stands or stood habitually erect. He had a cherry-colored, or strawberry, or so-called 'fire-mark' on left cheek."[267] Based on his and others' familiarity with Saul's appearance, Payne thought it comical that so many in Franklin County believed the man calling himself Ira Turner was Saul. "The idea that anyone in Rocky Mount not knowing Saul," he scoffed, "makes me laugh."[268]

Turner, however, bore a number of Saul's physical marks and characteristics. Although he was shorter than Saul and had lighter eyes and hair, he did have a similar facial structure. Saul had a scar on his knee from an axe injury. Turner, too, had a scar on his knee. The tip of a finger on Saul's left hand had been severed. Turner was missing part of a finger on his left hand. Also, there was a scar on Turner's left cheek in the same spot as that of Saul's birthmark. Was it possible that a surgeon had removed the mark?[269]

There were other questions surrounding the man's identity. Why did he think he was being held in Ashland for murder rather than a drunk and disorderly charge? Why, too, according to officers, did a man walk up to him and say, "Hello, Ed," in the Ashland train station? And why did Turner respond as if he knew the man?

Was this all a coincidence, or had Ed Saul, with help from the real Ira Turner or someone who knew Turner, taken on the identity of the jockey? C. Carter Lee seemed to think so and spent much time retracing the past movements of Ira Turner in Kentucky and West Virginia. What he found did little to prove his case that Turner was actually Ed Saul.

Finally, on September 19, during a preliminary hearing in the Circuit Court, Judge P.H. Dillard ruled that it was impossible for the state to prove that Turner was actually Ed Saul. His ruling was largely based on the testimony of ten witnesses from Rockingham County. Friends and family members, including his father, brother-in-law and cousins, all maintained that he was Ira J. Turner.[270]

And so, after three months in the Franklin County jail, the man who claimed to be Ira J. Turner was released. Returning to Rockingham County with his family, Turner hoped to reunite with the wife and children he had deserted some fifteen years earlier. Citizens of the county offered support for Turner, many pledging money and the offer of work to help him rebuild his life.[271]

The arrest of Ira Turner was as close as Franklin County authorities would ever come to bringing the killer of Marshall King to justice. And while the search for Ed Saul continued, he was never found. Ed Saul would never stand trial for the murder of Marshall King.

~ ~ ~ ~ ~ ~ ~

ON A DECEMBER EVENING in 1938, Mary Mitchell Derby and her husband Jack watched the road in the living room of their home in the western section of Franklin County. Suddenly, without warning, a shotgun blast ripped through the window. Fearful that they might be both killed, Jack and Mary raced for the stairs. But before they were able to get to safety, Mary collapsed at the foot of the staircase. Later it was determined that she had suffered a shotgun wound to her shoulder and the small of her back. She was dead within minutes of the attack.[272]

The Sheriff's Department, once notified, immediately came to the scene. But the authorities were perplexed by what they found. According to Sheriff Hodges, a 10-gauge shotgun with four unspent shells was found in the rear of the house. Nearby were boots and fresh footprints. The killer, they believed, had waited for just the right opportunity to fire the fatal shots that would kill Mary or perhaps Jack.[273]

The Sheriff's Department, however, soon turned its attentions toward Jack. Jack Derby had carved a name for himself as a daredevil driver for various automobile manufacturers. At county fairs and minor-league baseball games, Jack and his team of hellfire daredevils astounded crowds throughout the southeastern United States with their exploits. And as a well-known and courageous stunt driver, Jack earned the respect and admiration of the citizens of Franklin County.

But for many, including the sheriff, Jack was a suspect. Why, for example, did Jack Derby flee to the upstairs? Why did he not assist his wife who lay dying at the foot of the stairs? Was Jack somehow involved in the traffic of bootleg whiskey? If so, had he double-crossed someone, and had they, in turn, decided to retaliate with a shotgun blast through the Derby home? Or was there some sort of extramarital affair that might have triggered the killing? If this was the case, perhaps Mary was not the intended victim. In other words, was Jack Derby the target?

Despite the best efforts of Sheriff Hodges, his deputies, fingerprint experts from the Roanoke Police Department and a special agent from the FBI, they could find no clues that might lead to the possible killer. No one believed, however, including the sheriff, it was a random shooting. The evidence, it seems, pointed to a premeditated murder.[274]

While Sheriff Hodges and Commonwealth's Attorney C. Carter Lee eventually abandoned their belief that Jack was somehow involved, they did think that perhaps another family member was responsible. John L. Robbins, Mary's stepfather, they concluded, had a possible motive to kill Mary.

One month before the murder, Mary's mother filed for divorce from Robbins, charging him with cruelty and nonsupport. In response, he negotiated a settlement with her in which she would receive all of his personal belongings and his half of the forty-acre farm they owned together. In turn, she agreed to support him for the remainder of his life.[275]

But on November 29, she deeded, with the consent of Rollins, all of their personal property and the farm to Mary with the provision that she would support the two for the rest of their lives. A rift, however, developed between Mary and her mother, resulting in Mrs. Robbins and her husband leaving the home they shared with the Derbys.[276]

Lee believed that John Robbins possibly killed Mary to make sure he was provided for in his remaining years. This, together with his inability to provide a solid alibi the evening of the murder, convinced him to bring charges.

The case against Robbins, Lee realized, was weak. There were no eyewitnesses and nothing linking him to the boots, the 10-gauge shotgun or the four unexploded shells under the window of the Derby home. Fearing that Robbins would be acquitted if the case went to trial, Lee decided to nolle prosequi the charges against him. This way he would at least be able to recharge him if new evidence emerged.[277]

Robbins's defense attorneys W.A. Alexander and J. Brady Allman, however, objected and asked Judge A.H. Hopkins to allow the trial to proceed. They were certain that a jury would find him not guilty, thus preventing him from being retried for the crime. Judge Hopkins overruled their motion, and the charges against Robbins were dismissed. Much to the dismay of Lee, no new evidence ever came to light.[278]

Someone knew, no doubt, why those fatal shots were fired through Jack and Mary Derby's living room. But without any witnesses, the sheriff believed his best bet might be the boots and the tracks found outside the house. Yet without a suspect to provide a match for the boot prints, there was no one the sheriff could arrest. Unfortunately, Mary Derby's unknown killer had disappeared and would never be brought to justice.

Jack would later remarry and continue his career, appearing at baseball games, circuses and car shows. Some of the first recorded stunt drivers, he and his team would drive through a wall of fire with a man standing on the front bumper of the car. He died of natural causes in Hampton, Virginia, in 1970 at the age of seventy-four.

Chapter 10

DISAPPEARED

Eleven years after the Mary Derby killing, on a cold December night, Filmore Jamison sat down with his friend C.G. Richardson to have supper in his home in the Snow Creek section of the county. According to Richardson, a car pulled up, and the driver blew the horn. Curious about what the person in the car wanted, Jamison put on an army field jacket over his overalls and exited the house. Richardson was the last person to see Jamison.[279]

Filmore Jamison was a bachelor farmer who reportedly made moonshine and raised bright leaf tobacco, corn and wheat, as well as cattle and hogs, on his land. He, according to census records, was one of the largest and wealthiest landowners in the county, and as such, often carried substantial sums of money on his person. In fact, on the day of his disappearance, Filmore was said to be carrying at least $2,000 from a recent land transaction.[280]

Not long after Jamison's family reported him missing, Sheriff Curtis Ramsey and Commonwealth's Attorney Virgil H. Goode organized and directed an expansive search of the area near his home. Three hundred men gathered at Jamison's farm, and in more than one hundred trucks and cars, they probed every bit of ground and scoured every roadside within fifteen miles. They even drained a nearby lake but found nothing. And since the ground was frozen hard from the bitter cold, there were no discernable car tire tracks to follow. Soon the search broadened, and volunteers combed the banks along the Smith River from Henry County south to North Carolina without any success. Jamison and the car that had probably picked him up had vanished.[281]

The search, however, continued into 1951. But every tip or clue that the authorities received led nowhere. The authorities and Jamison's relatives feared the worse and offered $1,000 for the body and $2,000 to anyone who could furnish information leading to the arrest of the person or persons connected to the case.[282]

In an attempt to collect the reward, Betty Blaidsall and her daughter Bessie Crum in March claimed that Thomas E. Ramsey visited their house on the day that Jamison went missing. According to the mother and daughter, Ramsey told them that he planned to get Jamison into the car with him and steal the money that he had just gotten from the sale of some land. Witnesses, however, confirmed that Ramsey was working in Norfolk on the day of Jamison's disappearance. The mother and daughter were later arrested for giving false information to the sheriff and the commonwealth's attorney.[283]

Sheriff Ramsey had already arrested Alex Donovant, a Martinsville textile worker, for extorting money from Filmore's brother Lewis Jamison. Donovant claimed that a local fortune teller could provide information as to the whereabouts of Lewis's brother for a fee of $800. Donovant did apparently visit the woman but only gave her $100. When Donovant later met Lewis to break the news that she was unable to find the needed information in the spirit world, he was arrested and the remaining $700 returned to Lewis. Sheriff's deputies soon after retrieved the $100 from the fortune teller.[284]

A year later, in February 1952, a woman, whose name was kept anonymous, told Henry County sheriff Morton T. Prillaman that her husband, son and a relative kidnapped Jamison on December 18, 1950, and robbed him of his money. They then killed him at her home near Martinsville. Just how he was killed she never explained. But she did maintain that they dumped the body in a hollow behind her house and burned the body for two days in an effort to destroy it.[285]

Both Franklin and Henry County authorities took the tip seriously but could find no evidence to support her story. Jamison's relatives believed the tale she told was a lie. In her defense, she asserted that she had been afraid to come forward earlier out of fear of her husband. But now that she was seeking a divorce, she decided to share the story with her lawyer. Once again this was probably just another effort to get the reward money. This, like the bizarre tip they received from the fortune teller, shed little or no light on the case.[286]

But in August 1957, the new Franklin County sheriff, Ralph H. McBride, received a promising lead via long-distance phone call. According to the caller, a man told him that he was involved in the killing of Jamison and that he was buried in a wooded area near the Jamison home. By now the reward had been withdrawn, so perhaps there was something to this new lead. McBride and his deputies searched the area but failed to find Jamison's body. Jamison's disappearance remains unsolved.[287]

Chapter 11

BOOTLEG EMPIRE

The revenue agent pointed the pistol at Homer's mouth and pulled the trigger. The bullet shot out his back teeth and exited his jaw. Not realizing the extent of his injuries, Homer struggled with his assailant and pushed him into the still furnace. He then grabbed the other agent and threw him into the mash box. Homer would later be arrested, but given the circumstances, he would not spend much time in jail. The shooter had used unwarranted force and would resign three days later. Over the next few weeks, Julia, Homer's wife, would feed him sweet milk mixed with a little cornmeal until his mouth healed. It would be just one of the many wounds Homer Philpott would suffer from run-ins with state and federal authorities during the Prohibition era.[288]

~ ~ ~ ~ ~ ~ ~

THE PHILPOTT CLAN LIVED in Henry just inside the Franklin County line from Henry County. Born to John William Philpott and Mary Angeline Hardy in Henry in 1891, James Homer helped on his father's farm as a young boy. Tall and stout, he wasn't afraid of hard work or a fight, as those who crossed him learned. Although Homer never attended school, he was a quick study and learned to read and write.

Homer became determined to escape the financial uncertainty that plagued his father and most farmers in the region. At the age of twenty-three, Homer recognized, as did other enterprising men in Virginia, that the referendum authorizing the General Assembly to implement prohibition in the state would be a colossal moneymaking opportunity. And when Virginia officially went dry in November 1916, Homer was prepared.

Utterly fearless and with a head for numbers, he expanded his already considerable operations and established what could be described as a bootleg empire in Franklin and Henry Counties, employing hundreds of men and women to work as still hands, lookouts and transporters. By the end of World War I, Homer had twenty-three fully operational stills. Six of the largest were capable of producing eight hundred gallons of liquor each. He also had a fleet of twenty-three Buick and Hudson automobiles and $50,000, in cash, roughly equivalent to $860,000 in today's money.[289]

Unlike the many county men involved in the liquor business, Homer was something of a teetotaler. The sweet-mash whiskey his stills produced was good quality, but he knew too much of it dimmed a man's wits and could possibly kill him. "Liquor is a dangerous thing, and it's no good for a man; it will eat up his stomach," he said in a 1977 interview. Besides, he concluded, "it ain't made to drink; it's made to sell."[290]

Homer's expansive operations, however, got the attention of state and federal Prohibition and revenue agents, and in 1919, it all came crashing down. His stills, cars and sizeable fortune were all confiscated, and he would spend time in the federal penitentiary in Atlanta. It seemed Homer's career as a bootleg king was over.[291]

But it wasn't. Undaunted, Homer returned to making whiskey and would get shot a couple of more times, although not seriously. He had no fear of the authorities and would use whatever force necessary to protect himself even if it cost him his life. "I wasn't afraid of them," he later said. "I've got to die sometime." Referring to the revenue agents, he noted, "If he can beat me to my gun, it's his luck." But, "if I can beat him to his gun," he mused, "it's my luck."[292]

Homer would rebuild much of his empire and accumulate enough cash to purchase close to three hundred acres of land in the Brown Hill section of Henry by 1928. By then he also had the wherewithal to purchase automobiles, farm equipment and a sawmill that employed upward of forty men. When the Depression hit, Homer had the means to provide a good living for his family.[293]

Homer claimed that he quit making liquor in 1926 to focus on farming and his sawmill operation. Perhaps he did. From that time to his death in 1980, there is no record of Homer ever being arrested for making or transporting illegal liquor. This was not to be true of his oldest son. He would be in and out of jail for much of his adult life for trafficking in whiskey. But like his daddy, he would build a bootleg empire in Henry so large that he would make a fortune.

~ ~ ~ ~ ~ ~ ~

William Jefferson "Jaybird" Philpott was born in 1920 in the Brown Hill section of Henry, where Homer had settled with his wife, Julia Hurd Lovell. The eldest of four children, "Jaybird," as he came to be known for his talkative nature, was nothing like his father physically. Slight of stature and small-boned, Jaybird was the runt of the family. But what he lacked physically he made up for in bluster and bravado. Determined to prove he was the better man, Jaybird was never reluctant to pick a fight. And while he may have been on the losing end of many of these confrontations, he took pride in the fact that he gave as much as he got.

No doubt Jaybird's tough and authoritative father played a significant role in shaping his personality. Homer, as many of the folks in Henry recalled, was quick to use violence and verbal abuse to teach Jaybird and his brothers a lesson. William R. Martin, the former publisher of the *Martinsville Bulletin*, who knew Homer and Jaybird well, recalled an episode that occurred between father and son during a Sunday morning poker game: "Homer caught his son Jaybird cheating and he pulled out a big revolver and he shot Jaybird and you know what he said to Jaybird? He said, 'That'll teach you to cheat at poker on Sunday.'"[294]

Deemed unfit physically to serve during World War II, Jaybird decided to serve his country in another way. During and after the war, he began running liquor for Franklin County bootleggers. In 1946, he won some local notoriety when he rammed several police cars that were part of a blockade in Martinsville. While he was able to escape to North Carolina, he was later captured and brought back to Virginia to serve time.[295]

After completing his sentence, Jaybird's thoughts turned to settling down and having a family. In 1950, he married Katherine Ramsey and settled on land Homer gave him in Brown Hill. A raven-haired beauty, who hailed from Sydnorsville, she and Jaybird would have six children: Rita, David, Roger, William, Randy and Mary.[296]

Jaybird supported his large family by both farming and operating a grading company. According to those who knew him, he was a tireless worker. It was not unusual for him to get up each day at the break of dawn and labor until eleven o'clock in the evening.[297]

But the liquor trade was too profitable to ignore, and the adventure of skirting the law also had its allure. Soon, he was making liquor and running the proceeds to both in-state and out-of-state markets. As his profits grew, he expanded his operations and employed countless men, including his sons, to work his stills and transport his liquor.

Jaybird's liquor was very much in demand in the region. In fact, he often bragged that many of the lawyers and judges in Franklin and surrounding counties encouraged and supported his operations. Whether or not this was true is uncertain, but there is no doubt that Jaybird's whiskey was known to be superior to much of what was being produced in Franklin County.

Keeping his growing business undetected, however, was a challenge. Revenue agents knew Jaybird was one of the largest bootleggers in the county and conducted both ground and aerial surveillance of the Henry area. This required Jaybird to come up with a variety of ingenious methods to camouflage his operations.

One way he prevented one of his one-thousand-gallon-capacity stills from being spotted from the air was to bulldoze a large crater in the ground, build a still in the hole and then cover it with brush. County revenue agent Jim Bowman and fellow officers eventually found the still and blew it up, but not before it had produced thousands of gallons of bootleg whiskey.[298]

With the money Jaybird made from bootlegging, he was able to buy hundreds of acres of land, livestock and heavy equipment for his grading company. But there was always the danger of getting caught and having his assets confiscated by the federal government. To protect his financial interests, Jaybird made sure that all of the land and personal property he acquired was in Katherine's name. In fact, when Katherine filed for divorce in 1967, Jaybird had nothing to his name but his cattle. The house, land, equipment and automobiles were all legally the property of Katherine.[299]

While those who had business dealings with Jaybird claimed he was fair, they recognized that he had a dark side. He had an uncontrollable temper and could explode into a fit of rage at the slightest provocation—real or imagined. He was especially protective of his property. On numerous occasions, Jaybird assaulted unsuspecting neighbors who he believed had trespassed on his land.

In 1953, he shot George "Pete" Mullins in the leg and then beat him with a hammer in the mistaken belief that he had visited his still. Mullis had to have five operations to repair the damage to his shattered leg.[300]

He also threatened violence against local law enforcement. Jaybird once warned Martinsville police chief F.A. Gard "that if you ever come up on

Philpott Ridge, they'll have to carry you out." For these and other assaults and threats he became known to the Franklin County and Henry County Sheriff's Departments as "public enemy number one"—not just a notorious moonshiner but a dangerous man who was capable of anything.[301]

No one knew this better than Morris Stephenson, a reporter and photographer for the *Franklin New Post*. Morris's pictures and stories documented Jaybird's bootleg operations and his run-ins with the law. Incensed, Jaybird frequently threatened Morris. "You got yours's coming! I'll get you bumpy face," he often said in a cruel reference to Morris's pronounced acne.[302]

Today, psychiatrists would probably diagnose Jaybird as having an antisocial personality disorder. According to the American Psychological Association, such a person has the "chronic and pervasive disposition to disregard and violate the rights of others." Their behavior includes "repeated violations of the law, exploitation of others, deceitfulness, impulsivity, aggressiveness, reckless disregard for the safety of self and others and irresponsibility, accompanied by lack of guilt, remorse and empathy."[303]

Quenton Overton, sheriff of Franklin County, told Morris that he thought Jaybird might make good on his threats one day and gave him a small .25-caliber pistol to carry for protection. Stephenson, who carried the weapon in his back pocket, eventually discarded it. Better to die at the hands of Jaybird, he thought, than the embarrassment of accidentally shooting himself in the ass.[304]

~ ~ ~ ~ ~ ~ ~

As Jaybird's violent outbursts became more frequent, Katherine began to fear for her life and possibly the lives of her children. In August 1967, she left Jaybird and moved in with her sister Shirley Cannaday. In October, she filed for divorce, claiming that she was "forced to leave the home where she resided with the defendant, W.J. Philpott, near Henry, in Franklin County, Virginia, due to the cruel and inhuman treatment to which she was subjected to by the said defendant by beating, cursing and abusing her in many other ways." Yet despite Jaybird's promises that he would cease his abuse of her and the children, she maintained that she was in "fear of her life or bodily harm and for that reason, the said W.J. Philpott is guilty of desertion."[305]

In response, Jaybird denied that she had been mistreated and claimed that all of his assets were in Katherine's name and that he was unable to pay her child support, alimony and court costs. He further maintained that she refused to endorse a note to "enable him to borrow some money on which to support himself and family." According to Jaybird, Katherine had destroyed his credit, and so he must be permitted to sell whatever assets he had, largely livestock, to sustain himself.[306]

Jaybird also claimed that he had had a heart attack and that he was unable to work. His doctor, John Green of Ferrum, stated that he had suffered a coronary thrombosis and had heart muscle damage. The specialist who later saw him, Robert Crawford, said in a letter to the court that Jaybird was able "to perform only mild physical activity, and is not at all physically able to resume his previous very strenuous occupation as a farmer and as a bulldozer operator, in addition to other forms of hard manual labor."[307]

The judge, Langhorne Jones, was unimpressed. Jaybird was ordered to pay both child support and alimony. Katherine was awarded custody of David, William, Randy and Mary. Rita and Roger would remain with their father. She also asked that he be "enjoined from interfering with or in any way molesting your complainant (Katherine) and her children; that a divorce from bed and board may be decreed her and that the same may be merged into a divorce from the bonds of matrimony at the termination of the statutory period."[308]

The court granted her request. But the statutory period for the dissolution of a marriage in Virginia in 1967 was anywhere between six and twelve months. Katherine would have to find a safe place to live with her children until the divorce was final. Fortunately, her cousin Kenneth Ramsey said she could move a trailer onto his property adjacent to his house. Katherine was relieved. She believed that she had finally escaped the violent and impetuous man who one day might kill her and her children.

Chapter 12

DEATH COMES TO SALTHOUSE BRANCH

On the morning of February 22, 1968, Katherine Philpott got into her 1958 model Pontiac to leave for her job at the Bassett Table Company in Bassett. She was thirty-four, and it was the first public job she had ever had. She desperately needed it; the meager seventy-five dollars per month she received from Jaybird was not enough to sustain her and the children.

For the first few months of her employment, her routine was to leave her trailer around 6:00 a.m. and drive approximately one mile to Via's Store. The Vias were close friends of Katherine, and they allowed her to park her car at the store so she could catch the bus to Bassett. After work, she would take the bus back to the store and then drive her car back home. But in mid-February 1968, Katherine began driving her car all the way to work. She needed money and wanted to work overtime.[309]

The Ramseys heard Katherine's car engine that morning and also heard her drive down the road. But they became concerned when Dorotherene Cannady, her close friend and coworker, called and said Katherine had not shown up for work. She wondered if she was sick. Perplexed and a bit unsettled, they called their friend Bobby Whitlow, who also worked with Katherine. He too had not seen Katherine. Was it possible, they thought, that Katherine's car had broken down?[310]

They waited until 8:30 p.m. for Katherine to return home. When she didn't, they drove to her place of work and saw that the factory was closed and the parking lot empty. They returned home and called Frank Eanes, the

Katherine Philpott left Jaybird and moved into this trailer next to her cousin Kenneth Ramsey in Henry. *Courtesy of the Martinsville Bulletin and the* Henry County Journal.

superintendent of Bassett Table Company. Katherine, he said, had never shown for work that day.[311]

They then called the Franklin County Sheriff's Office and reported her missing. Almost immediately, John Price, the sheriff of Franklin County, organized a search team composed of deputies from his own department, state police and civilian volunteers. Fortunately, a state police plane spotted Katherine's car at the bottom of a five-hundred-foot embankment on February 24, four miles southwest of Henry just off Route 604 near the Salthouse Branch area of Philpott Lake.[312]

The car's transmission was in park, and the keys were in the ignition. Human blood was found on the inside front passenger seat. A pair of shoes that were identified as Katherine's were found in the right rear floorboard. Everyone feared the worst. Where was Katherine?[313]

Sheriff Price focused his attention on Jaybird. He was estranged from Katherine and was known to be a violent and vindictive man. Jaybird, however, maintained that he had no knowledge of Katherine's whereabouts and that he had been in Daytona, Florida, for the races when she disappeared.

Reporters from the *Henry County Journal* asked Jaybird to comment on what might have happened to Katherine, but he refused to make a statement. When they went to Homer's house for his take on her disappearance, Jaybird showed up and became enraged and assaulted one of the reporters. A warrant was filed by the reporter for "assault and battery," and Jaybird was arrested by a Virginia state trooper.[314]

In the meantime, Katherine's cousin Kenneth did some investigating of his own. On the morning of her disappearance, he had noticed skid marks on the road just below their house. He also had found one of her gloves in the same vicinity. On further inspection he found what he believed were signs of some sort of altercation: "There were also tracks which were made

Kenneth Ramsey discovered tire tracks and one of Katherine's gloves after she went missing on February 22, 1968. *Courtesy of the Martinsville Bulletin and the* Henry County Journal.

by the ridged soles of her shoes and signs there might have been a struggle. We also found a pair of men's sunglasses which looked like they might have been knocked off and stepped on."[315] Kenneth also found it strange that the two spare tires that were normally kept in the trunk of Katherine's car were found in a field below their house. Why would she have removed the tires?

But there were more puzzling questions. There was paint from Katherine's car on one of the fence posts near her trailer, and there was also a twenty-four-inch piece of fabric rope with a stain of human blood a quarter of an inch in diameter. Was Katherine bound to the fence post and then possibly killed?[316]

With the discovery of Katherine's car near Philpott Lake, Sheriff Price intensified the search in that area and called in rescue squads from Henry and Franklin Counties to drag the lake. Finally, on March 24, a civilian volunteer stumbled upon the partially decomposed body of what appeared to be a human female situated in a heavy thicket between two logs. No one doubted that these were the last remains of Katherine, but without verification from the state medical examiner, they couldn't be sure.[317]

Dr. Walter D. Gable, deputy chief medical examiner for the Western District of Virginia, was called in to inspect the body. Before arriving, he

Volunteers from the Franklin and Henry County rescue squads dragged this section of the lake near Salthouse Branch where Katherine's car was discovered. *Courtesy of the Martinsville Bulletin and the* Henry County Journal.

instructed Sheriff Price not to remove the remains until he had a chance to examine the actual site where they were found. Dr. Gable also asked that Morris Stephenson take pictures of the decomposed body.[318]

A young reporter at the time, Stephenson had never seen or smelled anything so horrific. After returning home that evening, Morris tried to join his family for dinner but the smell of rotting flesh was still with him. "In an attempt to rid myself of the pungent odor I continued to smell after entering the kitchen," he recalled in *A Night of Makin Likker*, "I took a shower and put on fresh clothing." Hoping now that he could enjoy the steak and baked potato that his wife, Sue, had prepared, he sat down at the dinner table: "I pushed my chair away from the table and stood up. As I retreated to the bathroom, I heard my wife vainly trying to explain to the children why I left the kitchen so abruptly."[319]

After returning to his Roanoke office, Dr. Gable was able to confirm that the remains were indeed, those of Katherine Ramsey Philpott. But

A volunteer found Katherine's remains in this thicket between two logs on March 24, 1968. *Courtesy of the Martinsville Bulletin and the Henry County Journal.*

how did she die? Numerous tests and an autopsy revealed that this was a homicide and that the cause of death was gunshot wounds. Not wanting to compromise the ongoing investigation, Sheriff Price and Dr. Gable declined, however, to reveal the caliber or type of gun used in the murder. They did state that they believed that she was not killed at Salthouse Branch but somewhere else.[320]

Sheriff Price and his deputies now began the search for Katherine's killer, and not surprisingly, their prime suspect was Jaybird. All of his property was in Katherine's name, and he had a motive to make sure she was dead before the divorce was final. This, together with his reputation for violence, convinced the sheriff and everyone in the county that Jaybird had either killed her or that he had contracted someone to kill her.

Katherine's funeral was at Mill Creek Baptist Church in Henry. She was buried in the church's cemetery on the hill across the road. *Courtesy of the Martinsville Bulletin and the* Henry County Journal.

When questioned, Jaybird still insisted that he was attending the stock car races in Daytona Beach when Katherine disappeared. Although no one could attest to his actually being there, the sheriff could not disprove that he was there. And without a witness to the murder or any physical evidence tying Jaybird to the crime, he could not make an arrest.[321]

And so the investigation continued well into 1969, but no new leads or evidence appeared. When pressed to explain why the case had not been solved after nearly a year since the murder, Sheriff Price stated that the "Sheriff's Department and the State Police, along with Dr. Gable will continue to investigate. No stone will be left unturned." He insisted that the case would be solved.[322]

Katherine's family and friends feared that her murderer would never be brought to justice. *Courtesy of the* Henry County Journal.

But Katherine's family as well as the public grew impatient with the progress of the case. Her cousin Kenneth and sister Shirley circulated a petition in Franklin, Henry and Patrick Counties requesting that Governor Mills Godwin bring the FBI into the investigation. The FBI said, however, that the murder was not in their jurisdiction since it could not be proved that it actually occurred at Philpott Lake, which is federal land.[323]

Throughout the remainder of his career as sheriff of Franklin County, John Price followed every possible lead that might turn up new evidence in the case. But each one proved fruitless. The case was still unsolved when he retired in 1975.

~ ~ ~ ~ ~ ~ ~

Jaybird spent no time grieving over the death of the mother of his children. On the contrary, on September 2, 1968, five months after the announcement of Katherine's murder, he married Doris Moss Milton in York, South Carolina. The couple returned to Henry and would live in the same house Jaybird had shared with Katherine and the children.

Why Doris would agree to marry Jaybird is perplexing. At forty-seven, he was bald, short and stoop-shouldered. He also was boorish and volatile.

Five months after Katherine's murder, Jaybird married Doris Moss Milton. *Courtesy of the* Franklin News Post.

Even more surprising, he was under suspicion for murdering his estranged wife. He had nothing to recommend him to women, it seems, except his bank account. But apparently this is what attracted Doris to Jaybird. He had the wherewithal to keep her in clothes, cars and expensive vacations.

The marriage was troubled from the start. Jaybird's jealous and violent nature led to numerous quarrels, and Doris suffered numerous beatings. Like Katherine before her, she feared for her life and left Jaybird only three months after they were married. Jaybird, however, demanded that she come back to him.

After learning that Doris was attending an anniversary party at a vacation house on Philpott Lake on the evening of December 21, 1968, he went to the house and forced her to leave with him, but not before striking the caretaker of the house, George Luther Whitlow, and Doris's aunt Elvie Mae Plunkett and shooting a hole through the living room wall.[324]

Jaybird was charged with discharging a firearm in an occupied dwelling and two counts of assault. After hearing the evidence, the jury deliberated only forty-two minutes and returned a verdict of guilty on all charges. The two assaults were misdemeanors and carried a fine of $500. But the shooting was a felony, and Jaybird was sentenced to twelve months in the state penitentiary.[325]

When Jaybird left jail in 1969, Doris was waiting for him, hoping perhaps that he had changed. He hadn't. The verbal abuse and beatings continued, and periodically, she would leave him for a week or two, only to return after he promised to change.

At times she reached out to the authorities for help. ABC agent S.A. Connor said she came to him asking for protection in 1973. She was convinced, he said, that Jaybird was going to kill her. Eventually, in 1976 Doris purchased a pistol from Alton Nunn, a Bassett Forks gun dealer. According to Nunn, "she said he wasn't going to beat her anymore." Despite years of abuse, Doris remained married to Jaybird.

Chapter 13

FIVE SHOTS IN SALEM

On the afternoon of Thursday, April 20, 1978, Jaybird stood on the concrete apron that surrounded the parts and repair building of the Carter Machinery Company at 1330 Lynchburg Turnpike in Salem, Virginia. It was a blustery spring day but a welcomed respite from the bitter cold the city and region had experienced over the past few months.

The company had had a presence in Salem and southwestern Virginia for some fifty years. Selling and renting Caterpillar equipment to coal mine operators, road builders, farmers and construction firms, the company had flourished, particularly with the development and expansion of the coal industry in western Virginia.

Jaybird was there that day to make a purchase. He needed additional parts for his grading equipment so he could fulfill his contract to run the Henry County landfill. Doris and their young son accompanied him, but they wandered to another section of the property. Jaybird waited to finalize the sale of the equipment.[326]

Jaybird was feeling particularly confident that day. Out on $75,000 bond for the stabbing death of Terry Flora, he felt certain he would be absolved of murder charges. And why not? He had enough money to afford two of the best lawyers money could buy—A.L. Philpott and Michaux (Shack) Raine. Once more, Doris, who was with him at the time, would not contradict his own account of the confrontation.[327]

But there was one problem. The fifteen-year-old girlfriend of Terry Flora, Denise Willis, had witnessed the altercation and the stabbing that resulted in Terry's death. Her testimony alone could convince a jury of his guilt and send him to prison or, worse, the electric chair. He was determined to prevent the Willis girl from testifying and had made it known that she was not long for this world.[328]

Denise Willis's father, Benjamin Bernard, known to everyone as B.B. and his wife, Vera, lived in Oak Level, just inside the Franklin County line. B.B., who drove a tow truck for a Bassett Ford dealership, knew Jaybird. On more than one occasion, he had rescued one of Jaybird's moonshine-laden vehicles from a ditch or one of the many steep ravines in the mountainous sections of Franklin and neighboring counties. He even pulled Jaybird's Cadillac out of a ditch one time after he wrecked trying to run down Doris.[329]

B.B. got little rest during the days and nights following Terry's murder. He listened constantly for any unusual noise outside the house and insisted that he know Denise's whereabouts at all times. He knew what Jaybird was capable of and feared the Sheriff's Department would be unable to protect her. He finally decided what he must do.[330]

For four days, B.B. followed Jaybird. At first, he wanted to just talk to him but concluded that any reassurance Jaybird would give him regarding the safety of Denise could not be trusted. After getting a tip that Jaybird would be in Salem at the Carter Machinery Company that day, he got into his truck and drove the thirty miles to Salem. On the seat beside him was a .38 pistol and a cocked and loaded shotgun. In the floorboard was a copy of a front-page newspaper article detailing the murder of Terry.[331]

As he entered the parking lot of Carter Machinery, he saw Jaybird standing in the rear of the building—cocksure as always and convinced that he would never see the inside of a prison. He stopped, opened the door of his truck and got out. "Jaybird!" he yelled. Unaware that Willis was armed, Jaybird turned to answer. "Do you want to see me?" he reportedly asked. "You damn right," Willis responded.

Not wasting any time, B.B. drew the .38 pistol from his pocket. Now seeing that Willis intended to shoot him, Jaybird turned to run. B.B. fired, hitting him in the back; Jaybird fell to the ground. It was then that B.B fired four more shots, this time hitting him in the abdomen and the arm. Jaybird Philpott was dead.[332]

~ ~ ~ ~ ~ ~ ~

B.B. waited for the Salem police to arrive and immediately confessed to the killing. He was unclear, however, about the details. Clearly dazed, he

Like Katherine, Jaybird's funeral was held at Mill Creek Baptist Church. He would be buried next to her. Many attended, said some observers, just to make sure he was dead. *Courtesy of the* Franklin News Post.

said that it seemed that the gun had fired itself. B.B. was placed under arrest and charged with the murder of Jaybird and taken to the Salem jail. But on Monday, April 24, B.B. was released on a $25,000 bond.

When friends, family members and the general public in Franklin and Henry Counties learned of the killing, they quickly rallied to support B.B. Having no savings and a mortgaged house, he would need money. Although B.B. never asked for help, people voluntarily organized a campaign to help him and his family defray the cost of his lawyers and the psychiatrists that would be brought in to testify to his mental state at the time of the killing.[333]

As for Jaybird, there were few tears. For years, he had terrorized the people of Franklin and Henry Counties, and most folks were glad to be rid of him. Later commenting on the case, one county resident said two years after Jaybird's death that "there were a lot of people who just figured that Jaybird was the kind of man who needed to be killed."[334]

Jaybird's sons, like their father, made and ran bootleg whiskey in Franklin County during much of their young lives. They are pictured here at their father and mother's graves. *Courtesy of the* Richmond Times-Dispatch.

Jaybird's sons were quite aware of the animus that citizens had toward their father and the Philpott clan. Roger Dale Philpott, in an interview at his father's grave in 1980, said that "the people of this county aren't going to be happy until me and my brothers are buried right here with our father." He concluded that "they're not going to be happy until the Philpotts are done and gone away with."[335]

Jaybird's funeral, which was at Mill Creek Baptist Church in Henry, was, by all accounts, well attended. But as family members recognized, most of the people who were present were only there to make sure that he was truly dead and had finally passed from their lives.[336]

After the casket was closed, Jaybird was taken to the cemetery on the hill just above the church. It was there that he was buried next to Katherine, the wife and mother he abused and perhaps murdered. On his tombstone is an epitaph that belies the violence and cruelty he inflicted on his neighbors and family: "My darling life was trust love beauty truth and goodness."[337]

~ ~ ~ ~ ~ ~ ~

FRED KING, THE COMMONWEALTH's attorney for Salem, did not want to prosecute this case. He knew Jaybird's reputation and was empathetic to B.B., but legally he was duty bound to at least bring a charge of manslaughter against Jaybird's killer. That said, he made no effort to condemn B.B.'s actions. Instead, he resolved to allow the community as represented by the jury to determine B.B.'s fate.

B.B.'s attorney, Jim Young, brought to the stand a host of witnesses, all of whom testified to the threat Jaybird posed to his daughter. Representatives from local law enforcement, including Franklin County sheriff W.Q. Overton, Martinsville police chief F.A. Gard and ABC agent S.A. Connor confirmed that Jaybird was a dangerous man with a long history of violence and brutality. They believed that he would, if possible, try to kill Denise. Residents of Henry also recounted on the stand how Jaybird had verbally threatened their lives and even assaulted them.[338]

To demonstrate the contrast between his client and Jaybird, Young asked witnesses to testify to the character of B.B. Unlike Jaybird, officials from local law enforcement said B.B. was a humble, soft-spoken man who had never been in trouble with the law. Bassett police chief Frank Vaughn said B.B. "would give you the shirt off his back."[339]

For most of his life, however, B.B. had battled alcoholism. In fact, at the time Terry was killed, he had quit drinking and was taking Librium, a prescribed drug used in the treatment of alcohol withdrawal. But Terry's murder and the threat to Denise's life caused him to relapse. More than likely, he had been drinking when he went looking for Jaybird at Carter Machinery Company.[340]

His attorney, Jim Young, painted a dark and brutal picture of Jaybird. Here, he said, was a man who was "subhuman…debased…sadistic." Citing the testimony of two psychiatrists, he maintained that B.B. had shot Jaybird out of an "irresistible impulse" to save his daughter. "You don't wait too long to kill the rattlesnake that is approaching your sleeping child," he stated in his closing argument.[341]

King asked the jury to reject Young's assertion that B.B. was not in his right mind at the time he shot Jaybird. The shooting, he argued, was premeditated and not the action of a crazed man. Jaybird was a threat to Denise, and B.B. killed to save his daughter's life. If they believed B.B. was justified, they would have to vote not guilty.[342]

In his closing remarks, King asked the jury to consider a verse from the Bible: "Greater love hath no man than to lay down his life for another." Was this what B.B. did, he asked? He then told the jury, "I leave that for you to decide; if he should be punished, and how much."[343]

On Friday, April 27, 1979, the jury returned a verdict of voluntary manslaughter, an offense defined as "the unlawful killing of another without malice, upon sudden heat of passion, upon reasonable provocation, or in mutual combat." The jury recommended a sentence of not more than twelve months in jail with credit for time served in custody. He was also found guilty of using a firearm in the killing, which carried a mandatory one-year prison sentence.[344]

The judge in the case, F.L. Hoback Sr., however, sent the jury back to set a definite term for the manslaughter charge and overturned the firearms conviction, which he said only applied to crimes of murder, rape or robbery. Both attorneys were satisfied with the outcome. Jim Young planned no appeal and was happy that B.B. would, in the end, spend only thirty-four days in jail. Fred King said he had done his duty, and the community had spoken.

Chapter 14

ROGUES' GALLERY FOR THE PROSECUTION

Sheriff Overton and Captain Wagner of the Rocky Mount Police did not believe James F. (Hank) Perdue and his wife Janet's story that they found Ivan Young murdered in his bedroom after they returned from a fishing trip to Smith Mountain Lake on September 4, 1978. Their suspicions were confirmed when Henry Housman, Larry Hudson and Hank's own son Bobby Perdue came forward as witnesses to the murder. The three claimed that they went to the trailer with another man the afternoon of September 4 to celebrate Labor Day. When they arrived, Janet and Ivan were at the trailer; Hank would arrive later.[345]

The group drank moonshine outside the trailer until it got dark. They continued the party inside until they realized they were about to run out of alcohol. Janet went into Ivan's bedroom to ask for money to buy some beer. Ivan, however, refused to give her any money. According to the three, Hank became angry, pulled out his pistol and said, "I will take care of this." He then walked into Ivan's bedroom and shot him three times.[346]

With three eyewitnesses to the killing, Hank Perdue's conviction would ordinarily be certain. But Housman, Bobby Perdue and Hudson were the worst possible witnesses that Commonwealth's Attorney Bill Alexander could put before a jury. All three were felons with numerous convictions for theft, armed robbery and assault. He would have to convince the jury that their story could still be credible.[347]

Before putting them on the stand, he told the jury about their criminal past and hoped that they would believe their stories. But this would prove to be a challenge. B.A. Davis and David Melesco, court-appointed attorneys for Hank Perdue, argued that the witnesses were unreliable and self-serving. Melesco told the jury that worse witnesses could not have been obtained "at a roll call in the state penitentiary." He maintained that the witnesses were like "three little monkeys that say no evil, hear no evil, and speak no evil."[348]

But he saved most of his invective for Hank's son Bobby. "What a prince he is testifying against his own daddy," he exclaimed. "Who was himself to touch the murder weapon, who took the guns, who sold the guns and who spent the money from the sale of the guns. Bobby Perdue." Bill Davis said that the "witnesses are the worst and the sorriest I have ever seen. They are the most reprehensible people to testify. Perdue's own son tried to sell his father down river."

When asked to make a decision, several members of the jury had their doubts about the reliability of Houseman, Bobby Perdue and Hudson. As a result, the jury was hopelessly deadlocked. The defense asked for an acquittal, but Judge B.A. Davis III refused and set a new trial date for February 26, 1979. Unable to make bond, Hank remained in jail.[349]

The second trial was, for the most part, a repeat of the first. The witnesses never wavered from their original stories. Hank, they asserted, had killed Ivan because he would not give him money to keep the party going. Bill Alexander agreed that his witnesses were a "rogues' gallery" of thieves and liars, but that did not mean their testimonies should be dismissed.[350]

In his closing argument, Alexander said that "it would be foolish for me to suggest that the prime witnesses in this case are anything but what the defense says they are. They are the worst people in the world to have to testify in a trial, but they still can be believed." Alexander wished he had "fine outstanding citizens of the community" to base his case on, but he was left with no choice but go with the evidence "regardless of where we have to go to get it."[351]

After deliberating for less than ninety minutes, the jury of eight women and four men returned a verdict of guilty of second-degree murder. Judge Davis imposed a sentence of twenty-one years in the state penitentiary.[352]

"With tears streaming down his face," reported the *Franklin News-Post*, Hank Perdue told the court that "the jury is wrong. I am not guilty. These men who sat on the stand know who did it. My son Bobby Perdue and Henry Houseman killed Ivan. I ask mercy from the court. I am not guilty." Davis and Melesco believed that their client was innocent and that he had been convicted on the testimony of "liars, thieves, rogues, stooges and little musketeers."[353]

Defense attorney Davis said that that "there is reasonable doubt in this case which is contrary to the verdict" and asked the judge to overrule the jury's decision. Judge Davis refused but told Perdue that he had the right of appeal the state supreme court if he so desired. He further stated that his court-appointed attorneys Melesco and Davis had waged a strong defense and could not be blamed for the verdict. "If you so choose," said Judge Davis, "I will move that they be retained as your attorneys on an appeal of the case." There is no record of Perdue initiating an appeal.[354]

Chapter 15

MURDER IN THE ORCHARDS

Boones Mill had, for the most part, been a quiet place. But in the mountains above the small village there had always seemed to be trouble of one sort or another. And it was on Arthur's Knob, an isolated community near many of the apple orchards in Franklin County, where Betty Lou Hancock was found shotgunned to death on a local man's doorstep. No one in the community knew her or could offer any reason why she had been murdered.[355]

For Quint Overton and his deputies, the challenge was to locate the two migrant workers who were last seen with Betty. Eventually, they found and arrested William Fralin, thirty-six, and Robert Dooley, twenty, both of Montvale, Virginia. After interrogating the two, Commonwealth's Attorney Bill Alexander decided to bring charges against them for Betty Lou's murder.[356]

Fralin, in an effort to get a reduced sentence, admitted that it was he who had fired the fatal three rounds from a 12-gauge shotgun into the back of Betty Lou. Why? He offered no motive. A Franklin County jury deliberated for two hours before finding Fralin guilty of murder in the first degree. He received, much to his dismay, fifty years in prison. Dooley would also be charged as an accessory to the murder and receive an undisclosed sentence.[357]

The killing baffled Sheriff Overton and Commonwealth's Attorney Bill Alexander. Betty Lou seemed to be harmless and posed no threat to anyone. Was her murder a contract killing, as some suspected? But if so, what could she have possibly known that would have warranted her killing? By all accounts, she lived on the street until she met Fralin and Dooley. To this day, no one knows why Betty Lou was murdered.

Chapter 16

A MURDEROUS AFFAIR

Sheriff Quint Overton thought about the carnage he saw at the logging site where Milton and Larry McGhee lay along with their friend Jimmy Moran and shook his head. What could have provoked those responsible to commit a killing this brutal? This, he thought, was not a robbery. Milton was found with a large sum of money. And from what he had learned of the McGhees and Moran, they were hard workers who were well liked and easygoing. They appeared to have no enemies. Once more, the crime scene showed no signs of a struggle. This was cold-blooded and premeditated. Overton and his deputies all agreed that they had never seen a killing quite as horrific as this in the county's history.

Bill McGhee had his suspicions. In fact, he told Overton that he believed that brothers Terry and Ricky Brogan had killed Jimmie Moran and his sons. They had been in the vicinity of the logging site a couple of times. Each time, they carried shotguns and claimed that they were hunting squirrels. Bill was so convinced that they were the killers that he told Overton and his deputies that he was going to kill them. Overton decided to bring the Brogans in for their own protection.[358]

It wasn't long before Overton concluded Bill was right. Shell casings found near the bodies of the McGhee brothers and Moran matched in forensic tests the 12-gauge and 20-gauge shotguns that the Brogans had been carrying. Waddings found inside the bodies were those commonly used to pack shotgun shells. In addition, Ricky Brogan's girlfriend, Norma Young, reported that on the day of the murders he had asked her to wash his clothes. They appeared, she said, to have bloodstains on them.[359]

Based on the circumstantial evidence, Terry was arrested on December 30, 1978, and charged with three counts of murder. Ricky was later arrested on January 5, 1979, on the same charges. But the case against both Terry and Ricky grew stronger when on January 6 and 9, Terry, in an interview with Sheriff's Department captain Jim Linnane, confessed that he and his brother Ricky killed the McGhees and Moran.[360]

After Terry's confession, Commonwealth's Attorney W.S. Alexander called for certification of charges against the Brogan brothers. After seeing the evidence, General District Court judge Joseph Whitehead found probable cause to certify three charges of murder and three charges of using a firearm in the commission of a murder to the grand jury. The Brogan brothers were now facing charges that would land them in state prison for the rest of their lives.[361]

After undergoing psychiatric observation at the Southwestern State Hospital, the brothers were deemed competent to stand trial. But by now, the evidence against them was mounting. In a letter to his wife, Glenda, while he was in the Franklin County jail, Terry not only confessed to an affair with Larry McGhee's wife, Karren Chaney McGhee, but also suggested that she wanted him to get rid of Larry: "I was too much involved with her. She said she did not like the way Larry slapped her and wanted a real man to take care of her. She said she wanted to have me by Christmas. She hinted that she wanted me to get Larry out of her life. I told her to leave Larry. I told her that if she wanted to get rid of Larry she would have to do it herself."[362] Karren, he continued, told him she "had a gun at his head one night when he was asleep, but I could not do it. I was afraid he might wake up."[363]

Although Terry denied that the murders stemmed from a love triangle, the evidence indicated otherwise. When interviewed by detectives, Karren confessed to the affair and even corroborated the contents of the letter. Sheriff Overton and Commonwealth's Attorney William Alexander were now sure that they had found a clear motive for the killings.[364]

Since both Terry and Ricky had confessed to the murders, it was not necessary to have a jury trial to determine their guilt. What would have to be decided was their punishment. Their fate would rest with County Circuit Court judge B.A. Davis III.

The courtroom was packed throughout the duration of the trial. Given the viciousness of the killings, the authorities feared that friends and family of the McGhees, including Bill, might try to kill them. The decision was made to search the witnesses and spectators before entering the courtroom.[365]

During the trial, Terry and Ricky changed their stories and said that the killings were an accident. Terry maintained that they had only gone there to talk, but when one of the log pullers suddenly jumped, his gun went off, and he shot Jimmy Moran. It was then that Larry ran at him, and he shot him in self-defense. Just why they would have then killed Milton was unclear.[366]

The facts, however, did not support the Brogan's claims. The killings, said Commonwealth's Attorney Alexander, were methodical. That the initial killings were an accident, he asserted, was absurd. "It was planned," he said, and "run through twice."[367]

Judge Davis agreed that the murders were premeditated, and on June 12, 1979, Davis convicted Terry and Ricky of three counts of murder in the first degree. Later on July 20, he sentenced each of them to three life terms in the state penitentiary. The two brothers, however, would be eligible for parole after twenty years.[368]

Alexander now turned his attention to Karren Chaney McGhee. Terry's letter to his wife and Karren's own admission to the affair indicated that she was complicit in the murders. She wanted Larry dead, and prevailed on Terry to kill him. Despite the fact that Karren claimed that both Terry and Ricky had absolved her of any responsibility, the jury found her guilty of murder as an accessory before the act. She was sentenced to twenty years in prison.[369]

In October 1980, Karren appealed her conviction to the Virginia Supreme Court. She and her attorneys pointed out that Terry had testified that she was not the reason why he and Ricky killed the McGhees and Moran. Further, even Ricky stated in court that he did not know his brother was having an affair with Karren when they went to the logging site. As for Terry writing that he thought she wanted him to get rid of Larry, this, they maintained, was just a flippant remark and could not be taken as evidence that she instigated the killings. The jury, they argued, had erred, and she should not have been found guilty of accessory before the fact.[370]

The members of the Supreme Court would have to decide whether "the accused was a 'contriver, instigator or advisor' of the crime committed by the principal." Five of the seven justices maintained that the facts in the case did not support the defendant's contention that she had nothing to do with the killings. Six weeks before her husband's murder, "the defendant repeatedly encouraged Terry Brogan to kill her husband. During this period, she informed Brogan where her husband could be found." After making two attempts, "Brogan and his brother brutally murdered the defendant's husband and two others at another logging site by firing shotgun shells into all of the victims' heads."[371]

While the justices acknowledged that Karren was not "involved in planning the details of the murders or that she knew the precise date upon which the murders would be committed," she still was an accessory. "On the basis of the evidence submitted," they said, "a jury could reasonably conclude that the defendant instigated the commission of her husband's murder, that she had reason to know of Brogan's criminal intention and intended to encourage his commission of the crime, and that her encouragement in fact induced Brogan to commit the crime."[372] The court rejected her appeal and affirmed the decision of the jury.

Chapter 17

A DEAL GONE WRONG

With violent and unpredictable Jaybird Philpott dead and Terry and Ricky Brogan now serving life sentences for the most brutal murders he had ever seen, Quint Overton hoped that he and his deputies might enjoy a respite from the killing that had plagued the county in 1978. But there were still two murders from that year that were unsolved.

Robert Alexander Newbill and David Dodd Hagerstrom, the two former Ferrum College students who were found shot and charred beyond recognition in a burned-out car, were now the principal focus of the department's investigations. But the two students seemed to have nothing in their backgrounds that would have led officers to believe that they might be the victims of some sort of run-in with local moonshiners or drug dealers. On the contrary, the two had no record of drug offenses or other crimes.

The investigation seemed to be going nowhere until Overton got a tip that Robert Lee Harris might have some connection to the killings. Harris, who was from Brunswick, North Carolina, attended Ferrum College until March 16, 1979, and had actually lived in a cabin in the area at the time of Hagerstrom and Newbill's murder. For three months, Overton traveled from New York to Florida interviewing potential witnesses. Finally, by late March he had enough evidence to connect Harris to Newbill and Hagerstrom to make an arrest. But Harris was now living and working in Cocoa Beach, Florida, and Overton would have to get extradition papers.[373]

After Harris was returned to Virginia and placed in the Franklin County jail, Overton and his deputies began the search for a second person of interest in the killings. The trail led them to Kenneth Lane Worley, a twenty-two-year-old carpenter who lived in Ferrum and was a friend of Harris.[374]

Worley said he knew nothing about the murders, but Overton had enough circumstantial evidence to charge Worley. After his arraignment in Franklin County District Court in mid-July, Worley had second thoughts. He was facing the possibility of a life sentence or, worse, the death penalty. He decided to cooperate.[375]

In a preliminary hearing for Harris, Worley, testifying for the prosecution, said that Newbill and Hagerstrom came to Harris's cabin the morning of December 10, 1978, looking for quaaludes. Soon after, they went with Harris to a pay phone at a restaurant near Ferrum. It was there that Harris made a call to locate drugs and later returned to the cabin without Newbill and Hagerstrom. Worley said Harris was angry that the drug deal was not successful and that he was going to kill the two men. Apparently, Newbill was also angry and had threatened Harris's life.[376]

Shortly after noon, Newbill and Hagerstrom returned to the cabin. Worley said he was taking a nap at the time and that Harris woke him and told him that they had arrived. Harris went upstairs while the men sat in the living room. When Harris came back down the stairs, he had a pistol. "Hey, Alex!" he yelled. When Newbill looked up, he shot him in the head. He then shot Hagerstrom several times, saying as he pulled the trigger—"That'll learn you to tell people you'll shoot me on sight."[377]

Worley said he agreed to help Harris load the bodies into Newbill's 1978 Mustang: "I was scared that if I didn't go along with him, I'd of ended up in that car, too." Grabbing a can of kerosene, he and Harris drove to a deserted road six miles south of Ferrum and hid the car in a thick pine thicket. They then poured kerosene on the bodies and watched them burn for a few minutes.[378]

Harris's trial for the murder of Newbill and Hagerstrom began in late September. After weeks of hearing Worley's testimony, together with that of Overton and his deputies, a Franklin County Circuit Court jury deliberated for seventy-five minutes and returned a verdict of guilty on two counts of first-degree murder. Harris was sentenced to two life terms in the state penitentiary.[379]

Soon after Harris's conviction, Commonwealth's Attorney Bill Alexander prosecuted Worley for his role in the killings. Although there was no plea deal for Worley's testimony against Harris, Alexander said the evidence indicated that his involvement was only after the murders took place. Worley, who was tried before a judge rather than a jury, was found guilty of accessory after the fact in the deaths of Hagerstrom and Newbill. He would receive a sentence of twenty years minus time served.[380]

EPILOGUE

The year 1978 was probably unparalleled in the county for killing. In the course of eight months, eight men and one young woman were dead. One of the men, Jaybird Philpott, many agreed, got what he deserved. But whether rightly or wrongly, by 1980 Franklin County had come to be known as not only the moonshine capital of Virginia but also its murder capital.

Quinton Overton and his deputies did their best to maintain order; however, as in earlier years, people in the mountains were reluctant to speak to the authorities, and violence still plagued some communities. Nevertheless, people respected Overton as an impartial and consistent enforcer of the law. By the time he retired in 2007, he was Franklin County's longest-serving sheriff, with thirty-two years on the job.[381] He died in 2021 at the age of eighty-three. His son Bill is now sheriff of Franklin County.

ABC agents Jim Bowman, Jack Powell, Ken Stoneman and John Hix, with whom Overton often worked, served equally long tenures trying to curtail the production of moonshine. Much to their amazement, despite the availability of good liquor in ABC stores, there still remained a demand for bootleg whiskey both in and outside the county. Many young men, including the sons of Jaybird, got into the business of both making and hauling whiskey. There seemed to be a never-ending thirst for whiskey from the county that had come to be known as the "Moonshine Capital of the World."

But what Jaybird's sons and other moonshiners soon learned was that the "uncontrolled flow" of illegal liquor from the county's hills and hollows had once again gotten the attention of federal authorities. The millions of dollars in lost taxes convinced the Treasury Department's Bureau of Alcohol, Tobacco and Firearms in 1979 to renew its war on moonshining in Franklin and neighboring counties. And after an extensive undercover operation, the bureau and the Virginia ABC Commission arrested fifty suspects and shut down forty stills.[382]

Ten Franklin County citizens, including brothers David, William, Roger and Randy Philpott, were indicted for operating two large still complexes and a sophisticated transportation network for hauling untaxed liquor to North Carolina and other states on the East Coast. Together they faced 120 years in prison and $130,000 in fines. Through a plea deal, the brothers served considerably less time in jail and received a significant reduction in fines.[383]

The federal government's aggressive approach, however, angered many respected citizens and even local law enforcement. "The way the federal people came in here shocked the conscience of the community," said one local attorney. The men they arrested, he maintained, were old-timers who had made whiskey most of their lives but were well known and respected in the county. "Franklin County is different than Washington," commented a county official. The men they charged "you could call up on the telephone and tell them what time you wanted them at the jail and they would show up. That's been a tradition here."[384]

As for the Philpott brothers, they had no regrets. Yes, they had gotten caught and would spend some time in jail, but making liquor was a long tradition in their family. It provided not only income but also a source of pride. It also had a certain mystique and pull that was hard to resist. In a 1980 interview, David Philpott stated that even if he had a more lucrative business "you'd still probably find me setting up something in the kitchen just so I could keep smelling white liquor." He concluded that "it's just something that gets to you and you can't stop it."[385]

~ ~ ~ ~ ~ ~ ~

FOR THE FAMILIES OF the victims of 1978, there was little that gave them solace from the tragedy of losing their loved ones. The Flora family sued the Philpott estate for the wrongful death of Terry. Keister Greer, their attorney, showed pictures of bloodstains inside Jaybird's Cadillac. Greer maintained that Jaybird did not act in self-defense: People, he said, "who behave in a lawful manner don't hide their cars. People who behave in a lawful manner don't hide their knives." In November 1979, they were awarded $600,000 from the Philpott estate for Terry's death.[386]

Doris Milton Philpott, Jaybird's widow, wondered how she was going to keep a roof over her and her three children's heads. Jaybird's estate was not worth $600,000, but she was counting on it to help secure her future. Acting as executor of the estate, Attorney Michaux Raine decided to bring a wrongful death suit of $2 million against B.B. Willis. But the Willeses had no assets, so there was nothing the Philpotts could possibly collect from B.B. and his family. They finally abandoned the suit.

Although estranged from Jaybird for weeks and months at a time during their volatile ten-year marriage, Doris insisted that her husband was not as brutal as people said he was. But she herself would soon come to realize that Jaybird could be just as cruel in death as in life. His will, written just three years before his killing, excluded her on the grounds that she had deserted him. She was to receive nothing. Once more, their infant children were to be placed in the custody of his sister, Lala P. McGhee.[387]

Doris, who was battling cancer at the time of Jaybird's death, was left destitute. She didn't have long to live. She succumbed to the disease in 1990 at the age of fifty-three. She is buried in Henry Memorial Park in Oak Level, Virginia.[388]

Jaybird's older children, who apparently had been at odds with their father, would also experience his posthumous wrath. David Kelton Philpott, Rita Dean Philpott Doughton and Roger Philpott were omitted from the provisions of the will. His younger children—Randy Philpott, William Philpott, William Jefferson Philpott Jr. and Mary Ann Philpott—however, were each awarded one-fourth of his entire estate.[389]

~ ~ ~ ~ ~ ~ ~

B.B. Willis in the end served only thirty-four days for killing Jaybird. Saddled with thousands of dollars in attorney fees, he needed to work as much as possible. A sympathetic judge allowed him to return to his job at Nelson Ford in Bassett as part of the work-release program.[390]

Following his release, B.B., with funds from his last remaining sister's estate, purchased his own truck and started a wrecker service, one that was capable of towing tractor trailers. But the allure of whiskey was never far away, and he began to drink heavily.[391]

Unfortunately, a stroke made him erratic and at times belligerent. Nevertheless, Vera, his wife of thirty-five years, and the family did their best to care for him. But one day while he was left alone, he managed to get a car salesman to deliver him an automobile. After getting some alcohol, he drove to Roanoke and struck a young woman and her infant son head-on going down Interstate 81 the wrong way. Thankfully, neither the woman nor the infant were seriously hurt.

B.B., however, did not fare so well. The accident left him with several broken bones and a fractured hip. His injuries, together with his alcoholism and addiction to pain medication, left the family no choice. He would have to go into a nursing home. He died at Franklin Manor, just five miles north of Rocky Mount, in 2002. He is buried in Roselawn Cemetery in Martinsville, Virginia.[392]

Many in the county would come to see B.B. as a hero; he had removed from their midst a man who had terrorized the people of Henry and Franklin Counties for years. Yet what he did on that April afternoon in 1978 was not some vainglorious attempt to achieve recognition but an act of protection for his daughter. B.B. was a quiet and unassuming man who simply did what, many believed, any loving father would do.

His daughter Denise, who was only fifteen at the time, suffered recurring nightmares from the night that Terry collapsed dead in her lap. She tried to recover from the trauma of that evening and return to school, but she could not bear the stares and whispers of her classmates. Although she was an honor student, she decided to drop out. Her mother, who had been proud of Denise's academic achievements, was saddened by her decision.[393]

While the nightmares ended over time, Denise did often blame herself for not doing more to help Terry. Sadly, she suffered from depression and often thought of suicide. But what could she, a young girl, have done? Jaybird was one of the most vicious and brutal men in the county, if not the region. Yes, she could have gotten the gun and perhaps shot him, but she couldn't find it. She did well to fight him off when he tried to grab the keys to the Jeep. She was fortunate that she wasn't killed that night.[394]

Denise, however, has not allowed the tragic events of that April evening to prevent her from having a productive and fulfilling life. She went on to get her GED and acquire an associate's degree from Patrick-Henry Community College. She married, became a mother of two sons and worked at a variety of jobs in sales and marketing in Henry County.[395]

Strangely, her husband, Tim Young, was connected, albeit indirectly, to the murders of Larry and Milton McGhee and Jimmy Moran. Tim's first cousin was Karren Chaney McGhee. His sister, Glenda, was married to Terry Brogan at the time of the killings.

Denise eventually moved to North Carolina and became a regional director for the American Heart Association and the National Kidney Association. Today, she lives in Hendersonville and oversees the Mountain Region for the Western Carolina Chapter of the Alzheimer's Association.[396]

~ ~ ~ ~ ~ ~ ~

HANK PERDUE, WHO MAY have been innocent of the killing of Ivan Young, would serve his time in prison and eventually return to Franklin County. He died in 2004 at the age of eighty-one. Bobby Perdue, the son who betrayed his father and may have been one of the actual killers, died at the age of sixty-one in Union Hall in Franklin County.

The Brogan brothers are at the time of this writing still in prison. Although they asked to be considered for parole in 2015, they were denied. The severity of their crimes, together with their lack of remorse and questionable behavior during their incarceration, convinced the parole board to reject their application.

Karren McGhee served out her term until 1984, when she was released for good behavior. Soon after, she married Kent Crawford Bennet in Chesterfield County. According to the marriage certificate, Karren was ten months older than Kent, and like it was for her, this was his second marriage. How long the marriage lasted is unknown.

What is known, however, is that Karren later married Earnest Weeks, a Franklin County resident. The couple currently live in Collinsville, Virginia, and have children as well as grandchildren. Despite the years since the October killings, Karren has remained silent regarding her role in her husband Larry's death. He, his brother Milton and Jimmy Moran remain the victims of one of the county's most brutal murders.

Robert Harris is still in prison for the murders of Robert Alexander Newbill and David Dodd Hagerstrom. Kenneth Lane Worley was released from prison for good behavior but died of natural causes in 1999. He is buried in Maple Grove United Methodist Church Cemetery near Ferrum. Just when, if ever, Harris will be paroled is still uncertain.

NOTES

Chapter 1: A Year for Murder

1. Denise Willis Young, interview by author, March 17, 2022.
2. Ibid.
3. Ibid.
4. Ibid.
5. Ibid.
6. Ibid.
7. Ibid.
8. Ibid.
9. Ibid.
10. Ibid.
11. Ibid.
12. Ibid.
13. Ibid.
14. Ibid.
15. *Franklin News-Post*, September 7, 1978.
16. Ibid.
17. Ibid.
18. Ibid.
19. Ibid.
20. *Richmond Times-Dispatch*, October 19, 1978.
21. Ibid.
22. Ibid.
23. *Richmond Times-Dispatch*, October 25, 1978.
24. *Franklin News-Post*, October 23, 1978.

25. Ibid.
26. Ibid.
27. Ibid.
28. Ibid.
29. Ibid.
30. Ibid.
31. *Franklin News-Post*, January 1, 1979.
32. Ibid.
33. Ibid.
34. Data taken from the *FBI Uniform Annual Crime Reports for the State of Virginia*.

Chapter 2: Hard Spirits, Defiant Souls

35. James G. Leyburn, *The Scotch-Irish: A Social History* (Chapel Hill: University of North Carolina Press, 1962), 99–119.
36. Parke Rouse Jr., *The Great Wagon Road: From Philadelphia to the South* (Richmond: Dietz Press, 1995), 21–51; John S. Salmon and Emily J. Salmon, *Franklin County, Virginia: A Bicentennial History* (Rocky Mount: Franklin County Board of Supervisors, 1993), 23–24.
37. Leyburn, *Scotch-Irish*, 256–72.
38. Bruce E. Stewart, *Moonshiners and Prohibitionists: The Battle over Alcohol in Southern Appalachia* (Lexington: University of Kentucky Press, 2011), 12–22.
39. Jess Carr, *The Second Oldest Profession: An Informal History of Moonshining in America* (Radford: Commonwealth Press, 1972), 17–22.
40. Leyburn, *Scotch-Irish*, 62–79; James Webb, *Born Fighting: How the Scots-Irish Shaped America* (New York: Broadway Books, 2004), 76–119.
41. Carr, *Second Oldest Profession*, 20–21.
42. See W.J. Rorabaugh, *The Alcoholic Republic: An American Tradition* (New York: Oxford University Press, 1979).
43. Ibid.
44. Stewart, *Moonshiners and Prohibitionists*, 24–30; *Richmond Times-Dispatch*, July 23, 1907.
45. Stewart, *Moonshiners and Prohibitionists*, 28–29.
46. *Richmond Times-Dispatch*, January 14, 1884.
47. Rorabaugh, *Alcoholic Republic*.
48. Stewart, *Moonshiners and Prohibitionists*, 40–48.
49. Ibid., 59–60.
50. Ibid., 64–73.
51. Salmon and Salmon, *Franklin County*, 397–98.
52. Ibid.; *Richmond Times-Dispatch*, February 23, 1884.
53. *Richmond Times-Dispatch*, February 24, 1884.
54. *Alexandria Gazette*, December 13, 1912.
55. Ibid.
56. *Shenandoah Herald*, April 18, 1890.

57. Ibid.
58. Ibid.
59. Ibid.
60. Ibid.; *Mathews Journal*, May 30, 1912.
61. Ibid.
62. Ibid.

Chapter 3: The Wettest Spot

63. *Richmond Times-Dispatch*, November 1, 1916.
64. Ibid.
65. Ibid.
66. *Daily Press*, November 10, 1916.
67. *Richmond Times-Dispatch*, November 1, 1916.
68. *Mountain Rose Distillery*, "Preparedness," 1916.
69. Hugh Harrington Fraser, "J. Sidney Peters and Virginia Prohibition, 1916–1920" (master's thesis, University of Richmond, 1971), 14–18.
70. Ibid., 19–24.
71. *Richmond Times-Dispatch*, February 27, 1931.
72. *Covington Virginian*, March 1, 1926.
73. *Daily News Leader*, August 13, 1920.
74. *The Bee*, May 1, 1922.
75. *Richmond Times-Dispatch*, July 26, 1920.
76. Ibid.
77. Ibid., August 13, 1920.
78. Fraser, "J. Sidney Peters," 41–64.
79. *Richmond Times-Dispatch*, May 2, 1932.
80. Ibid.
81. Ibid., August 13, 1920.
82. *Tazewell Republican*, March 18, 1909.
83. Neal Thompson, *Driving with the Devil: Southern Moonshine, Detroit Wheels, and the Birth of NASCAR* (New York: Three Rivers Press, 2006), 25–48.
84. *Richmond Times-Dispatch*, February 8, 1935.
85. Ibid.
86. Sherwood Anderson, "City Gangs Enslave Moonshine Mountaineers: The Amazing Story of How an Outlaw Group of Big Time Racketeers Made a Remote Virginia County the Wettest Spot in the U.S.A.," *Liberty Magazine*, November 2, 1935.
87. Sherwood Anderson, *Kit Brandon: A Portrait* (New York: Scribner Publishing, 1936; repr., 1985).
88. *Alexandria Gazette*, May 22, 1917.
89. Ibid.
90. Morris Stephenson, *A Night of Makin Liker: Plus Other Stories from the Moonshine Capital of the World* (self-published, 2012), 82–98.

91. Ibid.
92. Quoted in Salmon and Salmon, *Franklin County*, 409.
93. Henry Lee Law, *100 Proof: The Untold Stories of Notorious Franklin County Moonshiner Amos Law* (self-published, 2016), 90.
94. Ibid., 81–82.
95. Frank Mills, *Why Moonshine? Stories from Life* (Rocky Mount: Franklin County Historical Society, 2012), 45.
96. Ibid.

Chapter 4: Conspiracy

97. Thompson, *Driving with the Devil*, 19; Salmon and Salmon, *Franklin County*, 407–8.
98. Ibid.
99. Ibid.
100. Ibid.
101. T. Keister Greer, *The Great Moonshine Conspiracy Trial* (Rocky Mount: History House Press, 2002), 45–51.
102. Ibid.
103. Thompson, *Driving with the Devil*, 18.
104. Greer, *Great Moonshine Conspiracy Trial*, 132–39.
105. Ibid.
106. *Daily Press*, December 20, 1930.
107. Ibid.
108. Thompson, *Driving with the Devil*, 32.
109. Ibid., *Driving with the Devil*, 85–86; Greer, *Great Moonshine Conspiracy Trial*, 740.
110. Greer, *Great Moonshine Conspiracy Trial*, 635–740.
111. Ibid., 750.
112. Ibid., 741.
113. *Register Herald*, February 1, 2015; Thompson, *Driving with the Devil*, 237.
114. Ibid.
115. Ibid.
116. Ibid.; *Daily News Leader*, September 25, 1936.
117. *Daily News Leader*, September 25, 1936.
118. Greer, *Great Moonshine Conspiracy Trial*, 751.
119. *Register Herald*, February 1, 2015.
120. *Daily Review*, December 29, 1936; Thompson, *Driving with the Devil*, 218.
121. Greer, *Great Moonshine Conspiracy Trial*, 244.
122. Ibid, 845.
123. Ibid.
124. Ibid.
125. Ibid., 846.
126. Ibid., 847.
127. Ibid., 848; Thompson, *Driving with the Devil*, 227.
128. *Daily Review*, April 4, 1936.

Chapter 5: Thunder in the Mountains

129. *The Bee*, March 16, 1950.
130. Ibid.
131. *Richmond News Leader*, April 11, 1950.
132. Raymond Sloan, interview with Kip Lornell, Blue Ridge Institute and Museum Archives, July 7, 1979.
133. Ibid.
134. *Richmond News Leader*, March 13, 1936.
135. *Richmond Times-Dispatch*, December 13, 1979.
136. *Franklin News-Post*, December 13, 1979.
137. *Daily News Leader*, December 3, 1961.
138. Ibid.
139. Ibid.
140. Stephenson, *Night of Makin Likker*, 75–76.
141. Ibid.
142. Ibid.
143. *Richmond Times-Dispatch*, December 3, 1981.

Chapter 6: Mountain Vigilantes

144. *Roanoke Daily News*, August 19, 1897; *Richmond Planet*, August 25, 1897.
145. *Roanoke Daily News*, August 19, 1897.
146. David Hackett Fischer, *Albion's Seed: Four British Folkways in America* (New York: Oxford University Press, 1989), 767.
147. Quoted in ibid.
148. Christopher Waldrep, *The Many Faces of Judge Lynch: Extralegal Violence and Punishment in America* (New York: Macmillan Publishing, 2002), 21.
149. *Richmond Times-Dispatch*, January 19, 1905.
150. *The Bee*, October 21, 1925.
151. Ibid., December 1, 1925.
152. *Richmond Times-Dispatch*, December 2, 1925.
153. *Tazewell Republican*, September 10, 1908.
154. Ibid.
155. *The Bee*, September 2, 1940.
156. *Richmond Times-Dispatch*, December, 7, 1940.
157. *Alexandria Gazette*, June 29, 1903.
158. *Daily Star*, August 30, 1905.
159. *Stanton Daily Leader*, April 2, 1907.
160. *Evening Star*, January 28, 1880.
161. *Alexandria Gazette*, January 29, 1880.
162. *Norfolk Landmark*, September 11, 1903.
163. *Daily Star*, September 11, 1903.
164. *Alexandria Gazette*, September 11, 1903.

165. Ibid.

166. *Daily Star*, September 11, 1903.

167. Ibid.

Chapter 7: Bad Blood

168. *Richmond News-Leader*, March 2, 1860.

169. Beverly Merritt, "The Untold Story of the Clement-Witcher Feud" (unpublished manuscript, 2011), 11–14.

170. Ibid, 18–19.

171. Ibid.

172. Ibid., 22.

173. *Richmond News-Leader*, March 2, 1860.

174. Merritt, "Untold Story," 24.

175. *Richmond News-Leader*, March 2, 1860.

176. Ibid.

177. Merritt, "Untold Story," 40.

178. *Staunton Daily Leader*, January 21, 1905.

179. *Richmond Dispatch*, March 1, 1860.

180. Ibid.

181. Ibid.

182. Ibid.

183. Merritt, "Untold Story," 198–203.

184. *Staunton Daily Leader*, January 21, 1905.

185. *Richmond Times-Dispatch*, May 8, 1908.

186. Ibid.

187. Ibid., February 7, 1927.

188. Ibid.

189. Webb, *Born Fighting*, 32–101; Fischer, *Albion's Seed*, 621–42; Randolph Roth, *Homicide in America*, (Cambridge: The Belknap Press of Harvard University, 2009), 10–21; Bertram Wyatt-Brown, *Southern Honor: Ethics and Behavior in the Old South* (Oxford: Oxford University Press, 1982), 35–39.

190. *Richmond Times-Dispatch*, June 17, 1910

191. Linda Stanley, *Franklin County Killin': Murder in Franklin County, Virginia*, vol. 2 (Rocky Mount: Franklin County Historical Society, 2007), 41–44.

192. *Staunton Spectator*, February 7, 1882.

193. *Richmond Times-Dispatch*, February 28, 1902.

194. Ibid., July 2, 1902.

195. Ibid.

196. *Highland Recorder*, December 6, 1901.

197. *Richmond Times-Dispatch*, December 24, 1901.

198. Ibid.

199. *Roanoke Times*, January 13, 1902.

200. *Daily Press*, September 5, 1905.

201. *Richmond Times-Dispatch*, August 8, 1902.
202. Ibid.
203. *Norfolk Virginian*, September 8, 1880.
204. *Richmond Times-Dispatch*, September 12, 1902.
205. Ibid., September 7, 1930.
206. Ibid.
207. Ibid.

Chapter 8: Honor and the Unwritten Law

208. *Alexandria Gazette*, August 10, 1907; *Richmond Times-Dispatch*, August 10, 1907.
209. *Richmond Times-Dispatch*, August 10, 1907.
210. Ibid.
211. Ibid.
212. Ibid.
213. Ibid.
214. Ibid.
215. Ibid.
216. Ibid.
217. Ibid.
218. Stanley, *Franklin County Killin'*, 1–10.
219. Ibid.
220. Ibid., 6–7.
221. Ibid.
222. Ibid.
223. *Virginian Pilot*, August 4, 1900.
224. Ibid.
225. *Norfolk Landmark*, December 16, 1900.
226. Ibid.
227. Ibid.
228. See Thomas Keneally, *American Scoundrel: The Life of the Notorious General Dan Sickles* (New York: Double Day Press, 2002); Chris DeRose, *Star Spangled Scandal: Sex, Murder, and the Trial That Changed America* (Washington, D.C.: Regmery Publishing, 2019).
229. Ibid.
230. Ibid.
231. *Norfolk Landmark*, December 16, 1900.
232. Ibid.
233. Ibid.
234. Ibid.
235. Ibid.
236. Ibid.
237. *Daily News*, April 26, 1907.
238. *Virginian Pilot*, June 30, 1907.

239. *Daily Star*, April 23, 1910.
240. Stanley, *Franklin County Killin'*, 9.
241. *Richmond News Leader*, March 18, 1948.

Chapter 9: Getting Away with Murder

242. *Richmond News-Leader*, November 3, 1901.
243. *Alexandria Gazette*, November 5, 1901.
244. *Richmond Times-Dispatch*, April 29, 1902.
245. Ibid.; Stanley, *Franklin County Killin'*, 42.
246. *Richmond Times-Dispatch*, August 1, 1905.
247. Ibid., April 18, 1906.
248. Ibid.
249. Ibid., April 20, 1906.
250. Ibid., August 1, 1905.
251. Ibid., October 24, 1905.
252. Ibid., October 21, 1905.
253. Ibid., April 17, 1908.
254. *Staunton Daily Leader*, November 1, 1906.
255. *Tazewell Republican*, August 20, 1908.
256. Ibid.; *Virginian Pilot*, August 16, 1908.
257. *Virginian Pilot*, July 7, 1907.
258. *Richmond Times-Dispatch*, September 17, 1930.
259. *Virginian Pilot*, July 7, 1907.
260. *Richmond Times-Dispatch*, July 9, 1907.
261. Ibid.
262. Ibid.
263. Ibid., September 6, 1930.
264. Ibid., September 9, 1930.
265. Ibid., September 8, 1930.
266. Ibid., September 12, 1930.
267. Ibid., September 10, 1930.
268. Ibid.
269. Ibid., September 7, 1930.
270. Ibid., September 20, 1930
271. Ibid.
272. Ibid., December 17, 1938.
273. Ibid.
274. *Covington Virginian*, December 16, 1938.
275. Ibid.
276. *Richmond Times-Dispatch*, December 17, 1938.
277. Ibid.
278. Ibid., February 24, 1939.

Chapter 10: Disappeared

279. *Richmond Times-Dispatch*, December 24, 1950.
280. Ibid.
281. *Richmond News-Leader*, January 12, 1951.
282. *Richmond Times-Dispatch*, January 16, 1951.
283. Ibid.
284. *Norfolk Virginian-Pilot*, December 24, 1950.
285. *Daily Press*, February 5, 1952.
286. *Richmond Times-Dispatch*, February 6, 1952.
287. *Progress Index*, August 15, 1957.

Chapter 11: Bootleg Empire

288. James Homer Philpott, interview by Kip Lornell, Blue Ridge Institute and Museum Archives, 1979; Mills, *Why Moonshine?*, 52.
289. Ibid.
290. Ibid.
291. Ibid.
292. Ibid.
293. Ibid.
294. *Richmond Times-Dispatch*, December 30, 1979.
295. *The Bee*, February 26, 1946; Marjorie Quinlin, interview by Kip Lornell, Blue Ridge and Museum Institute Archives, December 17, 1985.
296. *Richmond Times-Dispatch*, March 19, 1950.
297. *Martinsville Bulletin*, April 23, 1978.
298. Ibid.; Stephenson, *Night of Makin Likker*, 67–68.
299. *Katherine R. Philpott v. W.J. Philpott*, Circuit Court of Franklin County, Virginia, October 10, 1967.
300. *Martinsville Bulletin*, April 23, 1978.
301. Ibid.
302. Stephenson, *Night of Makin Likker*, 76–77.
303. American Psychological Association, "APA Dictionary of Psychology," accessed February 28, 2023, https://dictionary.apa.org/antisocial-personality-disorder.
304. Stephenson, *Night of Makin Likker*, 77.
305. *Katherine R. Philpott v. W.J. Philpott*.
306. Ibid.
307. Robert C. Crawford, MD, to Judge Langhorne Jones, Circuit Court of Franklin County, Virginia, October 23, 1967.
308. *Katherine R. Philpott v. W.J. Philpott*.

Chapter 12: Death Comes to Salthouse Branch

309. *Henry County Journal*, March 14, 1968.

310. Ibid.
311. Ibid.
312. Ibid.
313. Ibid.
314. Ibid.
315. Ibid.
316. Ibid.
317. *Franklin News-Post*, March 25, 1968.
318. Stephenson, *Night of Makin Likker*, 79–80.
319. Ibid., 80.
320. *Franklin News-Post*, April 1, 1968.
321. Stephenson, *Night of Makin Likker*, 80.
322. *Franklin News-Post*, August 8, 1968.
323. Ibid.
324. *Franklin News-Post*, January 20, 1969.
325. Ibid.

Chapter 13: Five Shots in Salem

326. *Martinsville Bulletin*, April 21, 1978; *Franklin News-Post*, April 24, 1978.
327. *Franklin News Post*, April 24, 1978.
328. Ibid.
329. *Martinsville Bulletin*, April 27, 1978.
330. *Franklin News-Post*, April 24, 1978.
331. Ibid.
332. Ibid.
333. *Richmond Times-Dispatch*, February 18, 1980.
334. Ibid.
335. Ibid.
336. Ibid.
337. Ibid.
338. *Martinsville Bulletin*, April 23, 1978.
339. Ibid.
340. Ibid., April 29, 1978.
341. Ibid.
342. Ibid.
343. Ibid.
344. Ibid.

Chapter 14: Rogues' Gallery for the Prosecution

345. *Franklin News-Post*, January 29, 1979.
346. Ibid.
347. Ibid.

348. Ibid., February 26, 1979.
349. Ibid.
350. Ibid.
351. Ibid.
352. Ibid.
353. Ibid.
354. Ibid.

Chapter 15: Murder in the Orchards

355. *Richmond Times-Dispatch*, October 25, 1978.
356. Ibid., October 26, 1978.
357. Ibid., March 9, 1979.

Chapter 16: A Murderous Affair

358. *Franklin News-Post*, June 14, 1979.
359. Ibid., January 8, 1979.
360. Ibid., January 15, 1979.
361. Ibid., June 14, 1979.
362. Ibid.
363. Ibid.
364. Ibid.
365. Ibid.
366. Ibid.
367. Ibid.
368. Ibid.
369. Ibid., September 13, 1979.
370. *Karren Chaney McGhee v. Commonwealth of Virginia*, October 10, 1980.
371. Ibid.
372. Ibid.

Chapter 17: A Deal Gone Wrong

373. *Richmond Times-Dispatch*, March 26, 1979.
374. Ibid., November 16, 1979.
375. Ibid.
376. Ibid.
377. Ibid.
378. Ibid.
379. Ibid.
380. Ibid.

Epilogue

381. *Roanoke Times*, October 7, 2021.
382. *Richmond Times-Dispatch*, February 18, 1980.
383. Ibid.
384. Ibid.
385. Ibid.
386. *Franklin News-Post*, November 1, 1979.
387. *The Last Will and Testament of William Jefferson Philpott*, March 17, 1975.
388. *Franklin County News-Post*, November 13, 1990.
389. *Last Will and Testament of William Jefferson Philpott*.
390. Denise Willis Young, interview by author, March 17, 2022.
391. Ibid.
392. Ibid.
393. Ibid.
394. Ibid.
395. Ibid.
396. Ibid.

BIBLIOGRAPHY

Books, Magazines and Manuscripts

Alexander, Mike. "Moonshine Runners and Their Role in the History of Hot Rods." *Street Muscle*, August 14, 2012.

Anderson, Sherwood. "City Gangs Enslave Moonshine Mountaineers: The Amazing Story of How an Outlaw Group of Big Time Racketeers Made a Remote Virginia County the Wettest Spot in the U.S.A." *Liberty Magazine*, November 2, 1935.

———. *Kit Brandon: A Portrait*. New York: Scribner Publishing, 1936. Reprint, 1985.

Bondurant, Matt. *Wettest County in the World. A Novel Based on a True Story*. New York: Scribner, 2008.

Brundage, W. Fitzhugh. *Lynching in Virginia and Georgia, 1880–1930*. Urbana: University of Illinois Press, 1993.

Carr, Jess. *The Second Oldest Profession: An Informal History*. Radford: Commonwealth Press, 1972.

Denzendorf, Frederick C. *Wickersham Report on Law and Observance and Enforcement*. Washington, D.C.: U.S. Department of the Treasury, 1931.

DeRose, Chris. *Star Spangled Scandal: Sex, Murder, and the Trial That Changed America*. Washington, D.C.: Regmery Publishing, 2019.

Drake, Richard B. *A History of Appalachia*. Lexington: University of Kentucky Press, 2001.

Fischer, David Hackett. *Albion's Seed: Four British Folkways in America*. New York: Oxford University Press, 1989.

Fraser, Hugh Harrington. "J. Sidney Peters and Virginia Prohibition, 1916–1920." Master's thesis, University of Richmond, 1971.

Greer, T. Keister. *The Great Moonshine Conspiracy Trial*. Rocky Mount: History House Press, 2002.

Griffin, Patrick. *The People with No Name: Ireland's Ulster Scots, America's Scots-Irish and the Creation of a British Atlantic World, 1689–1764*. Princeton, NJ: Princeton University Press, 2001.

Joyce, Jaime. *Moonshine: A Cultural History of America's Infamous Liquor*. Minneapolis: Zenith Press, 2014.

Keneally, Thomas. *American Scoundrel: The Life of the Notorious General Dan Sickles*. New York: Double Day Press, 2002.

Kingsbury, Paul, ed. *Country: The Music and the Musicians*. New York: Abbeville Press, 1988.

Law, Henry Lee. *100 Proof: The Untold Stories of Notorious Franklin County Moonshiner Amos Law*. Self-published, 2016.

Leyburn, James G. *The Scotch-Irish: A Social History*. Chapel Hill: University of North Carolina Press, 1962.

Malone, Bill C., and Tracey E.W. Laird. *Country Music, U.S.A.* Austin: University of Texas Press, 2018.

McCarthy, Karen F. *The Other Irish: The Scots-Irish Rascals Who Made America*. New York: Fall River Press, 2011.

Merritt, Beverly. "The Untold Story of the Clement-Witcher Feud." Unpublished manuscript, 2011.

Mills, Frank. *Why Moonshine: Stories from Life*. Rocky Mount: Franklin County Historical Society, 2012.

Okrent, Daniel. *Last Call: The Rise and Fall of Prohibition*. New York: Scribner, 2011.

Powell, Jack Allen. *A Dying Art*. Vol. 2. New York: Press-Tige Publishing, 1996.

Rorabaugh, W.J. *The Alcoholic Republic: An American Tradition*. New York: Oxford University Press, 1979.

Roth, Randolph. *Homicide in America*. Cambridge: The Belknap Press of Harvard University, 2009.

Rouse, Parker, Jr. *The Great Wagon Road: From Philadelphia to the South*. Richmond: Dietz Press, 1995.

Salmon, John S., and Emily J. Salmon. *Franklin County, Virginia: A Bicentennial History*. Rocky Mount: Franklin County Board of Supervisors, 1993.

Stanley, Linda. *Franklin County Killin': Murder in Franklin County, Virginia*. Vol. 2. Rocky Mount: Franklin County Historical Society, 2007.

Stephenson, Morris. *A Night of Makin Likker: Plus Stories from the Moonshine Capital of the World*. Self-published, 2012.

Stewart, Bruce E. *Moonshiners and Prohibitionists: The Battle over Alcohol in Southern Appalachia*. Lexington: University of Kentucky Press, 2011.

Taylor, Joel Gray. *Eating, Drinking, and Visiting in the South: An Informal History*. Baton Rouge: Louisiana State Press, 1982.

Thompson, Charles D. *Spirits of Just Men: Mountaineers, Liquor Bosses, and Lawmen in the Moonshine Capital of the World*. Urbana: University of Illinois Press, 2011.

Thompson, Neal. *Driving with the Devil: Southern Moonshine, Detroit Wheels, and the Birth of NASCAR*. New York: Three Rivers Press, 2006.

Waldrep, Christopher. *The Many Faces of Judge Lynch: Extralegal Violence and Punishment in America*. New York: Macmillan Publishing, 2002.

Watman, Max. *Chasing the White Dog: An Amateur Outlaw's Adventures in Moonshine*. New York: Simon and Schuster, 2010.

Webb, James. *Born Fighting: How the Scots-Irish Shaped America*. New York: Broadway Books, 2004.

Wyatt-Brown, Bertram. *Southern Honor: Ethics and Behavior in the Old South*. Oxford: Oxford University Press, 1982.

Virginia Newspapers

Alexandria Gazette
The Bee
Covington Virginian
Daily News Leader
Daily Press
Daily Star
Evening Star
Franklin News-Post
Henry County Journal
Highland Recorder
Martinsville Bulletin
Mathews Journal

Norfolk Landmark
Norfolk Virginian-Pilot
Register Herald
Richmond News-Leader
Richmond Times-Dispatch
Roanoke Daily News
Roanoke Times
Shenandoah Herald
Staunton Daily Leader
Staunton Spectator
Tazewell Republican
Virginian Pilot

Interviews

Philpott, James Homer. Interview by Kip Lornell. Blue Ridge Institute and Museum Archives. No month or day listed. 1979.

Quinlin, Marjorie. Interview by Kip Lornell. Blue Ridge Institute and Museum Archives. December 17, 1985.

Radford, C.L. Interview by Rodney Moore and Eddie DeLung. Blue Ridge Institute and Museum Archives. September 20, 1976.

Rife, Earl. Interview by Patsy Mullins. Blue Ridge Institute and Museum Archives. June 6, 1974.

Scott, Myrtle. Interview by Wayne Bowman. Blue Ridge Institute and Archives. June 9, 1982.

Sloan, Raymond. Interview by Kip Lornell. Blue Ridge Institute and Museum Archives. July 7, 1979.

Young, Denise Willis. Interview by author. March 17, 2022.

Court Records and Government Reports

FBI Uniform Annual Crime Reports for the State of Virginia.

Karren Chaney McGhee v. Commonwealth of Virginia. Supreme Court of Virginia, October, 10, 1980.

Katherine R. Philpott v. W.J. Philpott. Circuit Court of Franklin County, Virginia, October 23, 1967.

Philpott, William Jefferson. Last Will and Testament. March 17, 1975.

INDEX

ABOUT THE AUTHOR

Phillip Andrew Gibbs is professor emeritus of history at Middle Georgia State University. A native Virginian, his ancestors have lived in Franklin County and the Blue Ridge Mountains since the 1750s. An avid cyclist and tennis player, he also works as a professional musician and is a founding member of the Georgia Midlife Chryslers, a rock, pop and R&B band that performs throughout the southeastern United States. He currently lives in Kathleen, Georgia, with his wife, Penny; their dog, Jack; and Moe—their three-legged cat.

Visit us at
www.historypress.com